MIND THE GAP

Unleashing Limitless Business Performance Through Organizational Capabilities

KIMBERLE SEALE

authorHOUSE®

AuthorHouse™
1663 Liberty Drive
Bloomington, IN 47403
www.authorhouse.com
Phone: 1 (800) 839-8640

© 2018 MTG Press, LLC. All rights reserved.

Cover Design by Kimberle Seale
Cover Image by Pitijopo
Author Photo by Kim Berry, Captured Memories Photography

No part of this book may be reproduced, stored in a retrieval system, or transmitted by any means without the written permission of the author.

Confidentiality and Anonymity: I have tried to recreate events, locales, and conversations from my point of view to convey points within this book. To maintain confidentiality and anonymity, in specific instances in my personal history, all names, company names, industries, products and service examples have been changed to protect the identity of those companies and their employees.

Published by AuthorHouse 03/14/2018

ISBN: 978-1-5462-2862-2 (sc)
ISBN: 978-1-5462-2860-8 (hc)
ISBN: 978-1-5462-2861-5 (e)

Library of Congress Control Number: 2018901913

Print information available on the last page.

Any people depicted in stock imagery provided by Getty Images are models, and such images are being used for illustrative purposes only.
Certain stock imagery © Getty Images.

This book is printed on acid-free paper.

Because of the dynamic nature of the Internet, any web addresses or links contained in this book may have changed since publication and may no longer be valid. The views expressed in this work are solely those of the author and do not necessarily reflect the views of the publisher, and the publisher hereby disclaims any responsibility for them.

This book is dedicated to my husband, children, and parents who have provided me endless support and inspired me to put my thoughts on paper

Contents

Mind The Gap xiii
Recognizing You Have a Problem 1
Start with the List 3
Strategic Focus 7
Leadership 17
Talent 31
Domain Expertise 41
Productivity 51
Continuous Learning 59
Innovation 67
Brand Identity 75
Collaboration 83
Customer Intimacy 91
Customer Service 99
Speed and Agility 107
Quality 115
Enabling Technology 125
Strategic Partnerships 131
Effective Communication 137
Values 145
Don't Let Your Culture Eat Your Strategy For Lunch! 157
Kimberle Seale 179

Acknowledgements

I just want to say thank you to all those that have been pivotal in why I am where I am today and helped made this book a reality and a success.

David Bartley
Rubi Ho
Heather Cassady
Scot Montgomery
George Reed
Eileen McGovern
Andy Stewart
Mitch Scobell
Missy Nack
Jeff Ton
Lynn Buckland
Stefano Malnati
Jonathan Polak
Scott Dinwiddie
Seth Rhoades
John G.
Julie Sterle
Jan Johnson
David Wieczorek
Jo Biggers
Shane Irving
Tony R.
Andrea Butcher
Mike Kelly
Cindy Booth
Julie Kennedy
Amy Shackle
Doug Heath
George Saich
Tom Wood
Ron F.
Melissa Norcross
Patrick Farran

Preface

For many years, I originally thought I missed my calling. I believed I should have been a Doctor. With how much I enjoy science, understanding, and helping people be healthy, I took the wrong road. At least, so I thought. However, after the many years when I would drive through the IU Medical Center campus and yearn to be in scrubs, I continued my study and maturing of organizational capabilities. It finally dawned on me I was still practicing my passion for understanding and helping people through organizational health, and I didn't need scrubs to do that.

In 2016, my husband, Adam and I were discussing the information I had used as my "playbook" over the years. I had been feeling a little nervous about a power loss with one of our backup systems where most of my information resided. This pile of information was in the form of books, examples, ideas, case studies, and websites all linked to one common theme. This common theme all connected in my head and was difficult to explain. With some leaders that have attention deficit, it was really hard to explain in seven seconds. I had this approach to uncovering pain, assessing, and utilizing various techniques to improve business performance, but I was unable to communicate it in such a way that it would resonate. At one point, Adam said, "Why don't you write it all down?"

Fast forward to 2017; I remember the day very well, it was October 18th, and I am having after work drinks with colleagues when one of them recommended I read the book by Honorée Corder called *You Must Write A Book*. And that was when *Mind The Gap* really began.

Those that would benefit from this book the most would be:

- The Leader who knows something is not working as it should
- The HR professional who needs to know how to assess the situation and get started
- The business owner who needs to increase sales, improve expenses and net income, or lay the foundation for a higher sales price for their company

The second book in this series will be for the leaders and their employees to "Mind The Gap" in their professional and personal lives.

Introduction

Mind The Gap

Remember that old cliché "Culture eats strategy for lunch?" What does that really mean? Let's take a look at some statistics, and when you look under the cover, whatever word you may choose, your company culture will determine your success.

Company success statistics are staggering:

- 87% of companies fail to execute their strategy successfully because of a lack of trust, communication, and collaboration with leadership.[4] In a Forbes study, 92% of CEOs indicate communication is integral to successfully execute their strategy.[5]
- 8% of leaders are effective at both strategy and execution. That means there are 92% effective only in strategy, execution, or neither.[6]
- 80% of businesses fail within the first 18 months.[3]

Levels of employee engagement make the success of your strategy even more difficult:

- In 2013, studies showed 13% of the world's workers were actively engaged at work[1], and that number has improved very little since then.
- As of December 2017, 85% of employees worldwide are not engaged, meaning they lack motivation and are less likely to invest extra effort in organizational goals or outcomes. 18% are "actively disengaged," indicating they are unhappy and unproductive and liable to spread negativity to coworkers.[9] Just imagine, every sixth person that walks by you may want to have a few minutes of your time to complain? Or they have been coming late to work? Or is spending their time surfing the web? Or doing anything else to avoid working?
- 38% productivity: 2 hours and 53 minutes out of 8 hours is the amount of time the average worker is productive.[2] Other studies by

the Department of Labor show the number to be 3 out of 8 hours. Although these are two completely different studies, they differ by only 7 minutes. That means that the $50,000/year worker you pay is only giving you $19,000 of productivity.
- If you look at the 85% who are not engaged and the 38% productivity statistics, it's no wonder there is an approximate loss of $7 trillion in productivity costs for the year.[9]
- In 2020, the freelance workforce (a.k.a. the Gig Economy) is predicted to rise to 43%.[8]
- Half of today's workforce could be automated by 2055, but that could happen earlier. 60% of occupations have at least 30% of their activities that could be automated.[7]

How do companies prepare and create a competitive advantage for a sustainable future with the challenge of these statistics above? Do you have something that is rare or unique that no one can duplicate? Does your organization deliver your products and services better than other organizations? Are you prepared for the Gig Economy and the impacts of automation on the future of your workforces?

Every organization has a problem, or many, that creates a gap in performance. And the deeper you go in your strategy, the harder that gap is to understand and fix. Many leaders will focus on what looks easy or the surface symptoms only to then miss the true cause thereby wasting time and effort. For example, if revenue is dropping because you are losing customers to a competitor, you may find ways to get new customers or lower your prices to keep the ones you have. These solutions may work as a temporary fix. However, the deeper you dig, you may find the cause is attributed to poor customer service or quality. That poor service and quality may be due to a lack of talent, knowledge, or some other factors.

So, the question becomes, how do you "mind the gap" and create a strategic foundation for your company that accomplishes three primary goals:

1. Differentiates
2. Is difficult for competitors to emulate
3. Provides the ability to grow

The remainder of this book focuses on defining, diagnosing, and building measurable organizational capabilities based on the needs of your company that accomplish these primary goals.

But, before we get started, let's explore what organizational capabilities are. These are going to be the indestructible bricks in your organization's foundation that prevent gaps in performance.

Think of these bricks as a collective-set of skills and expertise coupled with the culture or behaviors of an organization. They represent the collective way your resources work together, across the entire organization. Their maturity can make or break your success. The cliché "culture eats strategy for lunch" is, in fact, a reality.

This foundation is your organization's DNA that defines what you are good at doing. This DNA is invisible to the naked eye. You can't see or touch it. It is difficult to measure, emulate, and even cure but is required to drive the success of any organization. These foundational bricks or DNA can be compared to the simple hierarchy of human needs. These bricks are the air, food, drink, warmth, sleep, shelter, security, freedom from fear, trust, acceptance, and need for respect. Until you have this foundation built throughout, you can't move on to higher levels that realize the full potential and experience peak peak performance, as you would with the self-actualization for a human.

Have you ever experienced any of the following?

- a large amount of fear from your employees
- lack of accountability
- finger pointing or CYA
- long delays to get something done that, in reality, shouldn't be that difficult
- too many number-one priorities
- silos
- lack of the right talent and leadership
- lack of use of best practices
- an excess of manual processes
- lots of activity but no results

Maybe you have experienced a few of them, all of them, or your list is longer? Something within your organization's DNA is not functioning well; you have a gap in your foundation. And when the organization is unhealthy, it affects everything you do.

This example is no different than when you, yourself, are unhealthy. Such as, when you have an infection with a 104° temperature. You can't see the bug inside of you; you can only see, hear, and feel the symptoms. Most will treat the fever with Tylenol. However, if you don't treat the infection with antibiotics your symptoms won't go away, and you will get worse. Additionally, these symptoms impact your ability to function normally or work. How well do you communicate when you are this sick? How well do you plan or execute an activity? How often do you want to just go back to bed?

The following chapters will explain an approach to "Mind the Gap" for your organization. This approach identifies ways to repair the gap you have today in your foundation and unleashes limitless performance by improving your organizational capabilities. The capabilities with which you identify, represent the identity of who your organization "is," as perceived by your employees, customers, stakeholders, etc. These capabilities will enable your organization to delight your customers, outperform competitors, and dominate your markets. Through their continued evaluation and strengthening, these organizational capabilities will become increasingly more difficult, if not impossible, for any competitor to understand and emulate, providing the organization the foundation for sustainable growth.

Chapter 1

Recognizing You Have a Problem

Many companies are plagued with organizational problems. These may be localized to a department, a team, individual or could be systemic across the entire organization. Within this book, we will discuss stories from various companies and their organizational problems. We will then identify the missing organizational capabilities these align with and solutions on a path to success.

It's important to note; there are entire companies that focus just on one or more of these capabilities as a part of their business. This book is not meant to be all-inclusive or exhaustive. Only a simple "temperature gauge" as to whether or not you have a problem that needs further attention with direction on where to begin. Within the reference section, there are listed other related resources to help you go deeper if desired.

What follows are three company examples from my past we will reference from time to time in this book. To illustrate some of these concepts, here's a little background to help you understand better.

Palentine

The first of the three companies, Palentine, was a product and services provider for healthcare companies. Palentine had undergone a change in the executive leadership required to move the company into a strategic buy situation for their shareholders.

The new leadership that came into the company replaced the existing executives and were responsible for improving the revenue and bottom line.

Based on the approach of the new leadership to reduce costs, Palentine experienced their first ever downsizing. This event set the tone and speed of trajectory for the next few years into a downward spiral of fear, lack of ownership, lack of trust and respect, and ultimately customer dissatisfaction and loss.

Neolistics

Neolistics was a small software start-up providing products to the financial services industry. As with many start-ups, the first few years were fast and furious as they spun up new customers. During this time, the company became quite manually intensive in the process. They didn't keep up with necessary changes to their technology over the years and instead maintained focus on growing the business. Overall, this company was suffering from not understanding their direction while the biggest complaints by the employees were there was too much work to do and not knowing where to focus their time.

Baltic

Baltic was a product and services provider for the manufacturing industry. The company had recently purchased and merged two of its largest acquisitions and was executing plans to cut costs, and integrate the two companies. As a symptomatic result of the cost-cutting strategy, the behaviors of the employees were toxic. There were numerous complaints, low satisfaction, little accountability, little innovation, and high frustration levels accompanied with turnover. This company also began to experience major quality issues with the products they sold after the downsizing occurred, which ultimately led to the company bleeding revenue.

Chapter 2

Start with the List

There is no easy answer as to which capabilities every organization should have. However, you will see similarities in good companies. Your organization should excel in a few of these and at least do well in the rest. For example, Google excels in innovation as an organizational capability, with core competencies of search engine optimization algorithms and data warehousing, that has created a competitive advantage for the company.

Below is the list of organizational capabilities this book will address. The wording of each may be a little different for every organization, so a few synonyms are listed next to the capabilities.

1. Customer Service (Customer Care or Experience)
2. Brand Identity (Brand Awareness)
3. Customer Intimacy
4. Quality
5. Innovation (Think Tank)
6. Speed & Agility (Fast, Time to Market)
7. Productivity (Execution)
8. Enabling Technology
9. Strategic Focus (Strategic Execution)
10. Domain Expertise (Subject Matter Expertise, Business Acumen)
11. Talent (People)
12. Strategic Partnerships (Vendor Management)
13. Continuous Learning (Process Improvement)
14. Collaboration (Teamwork)
15. Leadership
16. Effective Communication
17. Values

This is a long list. Which capabilities should have your organization's focus? Which ones should you excel at, or just be good? Collectively, all are daunting and having too many will be destabilizing. There is no magic number, so select those that have importance for you. Take a look at your vision, mission, and goals, then decide what capabilities are the most critical? You may find capabilities as the exact words in your vision or mission statements. Take a look at what your customers expect most from what your business offers. Is it quality or maybe customer service? Next, review the expectations of your processes and the people you require to deliver your vision and customer expectations.

There you have it: your list.

The following is an Organizational Capability Map of how these capabilities work together in a set of themes (Values, People, Process, Products & Services, and Customer that ultimately lead to generating revenue and net income). A lower-level capability may be the cause of a symptom you see in a higher-level capability. Strong connections between the ovals are represented by the arrow that points to the next oval that could be the "infection" causing your symptoms.

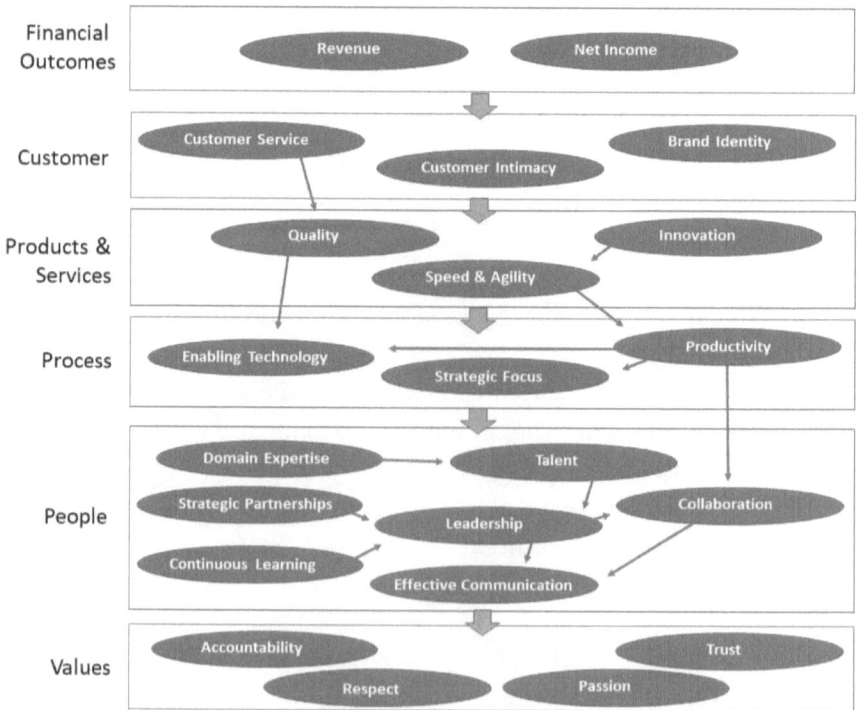

For example, if you detect symptoms that your Productivity output (above within the Process theme) is not meeting your targets, take a look to see if you have the maturity in Enabling Technology and Strategic Focus to be productive. An entire theme is important as well. If your talent is exiting your organization faster than you can hire, take a look at the impact of your leadership, as well as, the effectiveness of collaboration and communication. If these capabilities aren't as effective as they should be, go deeper and evaluate the values theme. Does your leadership struggle with effective values?

As another example higher up on the map, if your customers are complaining more than normal, how effective is your Customer Service? And how about the Quality, Speed & Agility, and Innovation of your products and services? Are these capabilities meeting your or your customers' expectations?

Now, if you are still struggling with which capabilities you need to select and which you must excel at, I will give you an early hint. There are three that you need to mature and excel at first; then the rest will come easier and faster. It is the exponential power of these three, where failure within them, your efforts will be costly.

Chapter 3

Strategic Focus

"The essence of strategy is choosing what not to do." - Michael Porter, known for his theories on economics and business strategy.

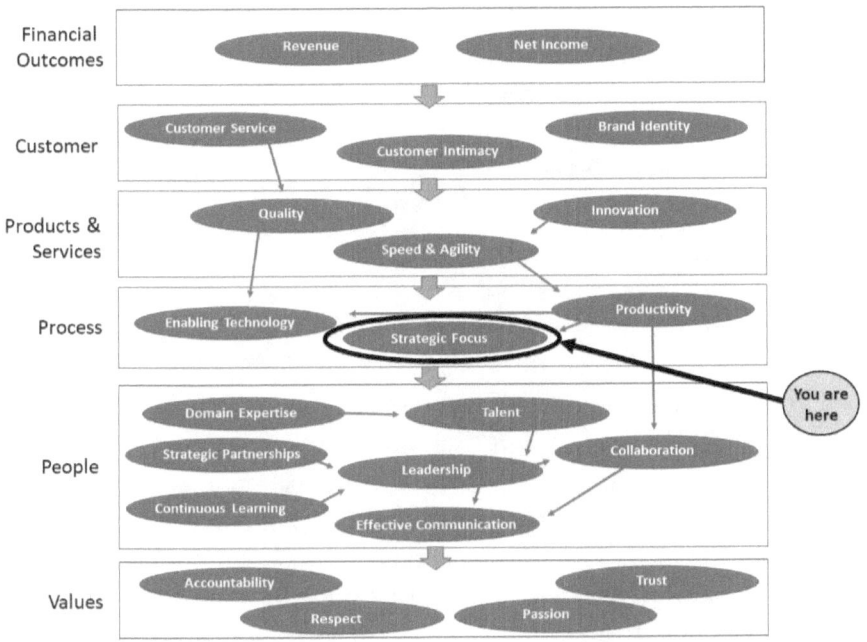

The Vision:

We hold ourselves accountable for flawlessly articulating, executing, and aligning to a single, strategic direction that is both achievable and stretches the organization to accomplish the intended outcomes.

What the Data Says:

- 87% of companies fail to execute their strategy successfully because of a lack of trust, communication, and collaboration with leadership.[5] In a Forbes study, 92% of CEOs indicate communication is integral to successfully execute their strategy.[3]
- 8% of leaders are effective at both strategy and execution. That means there are 92% effective only in strategy, execution, or neither.[2]
- When taking on a new C-Suite role, executives ranked "creating a shared vision and alignment around strategic direction across the organization" as the most important transition activity.[1]
- Companies experienced a gap between expectations and performance and only achieved 63% of the expected results of their strategic plans.[4]

The Meaning:

Originally, I had Strategic Focus and Execution as two separate capabilities. However, the more I wrote this book, the more I just couldn't separate the two. You just can't have one without the other and still be successful. You can have a focused strategy, but what's the point if you can't execute it? I have also seen companies that are great at project management and can execute a project on budget, on schedule, and sometimes even deliver on the business expectations. But without a good strategy, you could be wasting time and money on irrelevant efforts that don't move your organization forward.

Companies that apply a consistent set of best practices where the following are in place gain significant results and outpace their competitors:

- a collective vision;
- the strategy is established and translated;
- the organization is aligned and understands the strategy from top to bottom and bottom to top;
- the strategy is planned and budgeted for execution;
- a governance structure is in place to review, test, and the strategy is adapted.

Examples:

Below are a few company examples of setbacks, success stories, and turnarounds where Strategic Focus was mature or missing.

Company: Federal Express (now FedEx Corp.)

The Setback and Refocus: After transforming overnight shipping in 1971, Fred Smith continued to innovate with a competitive fax machine product. In 1983 FedEx hit $1B in revenue. Then Smith introduced an electronic delivery service called Zapmail in 1984, image-processing equipment that produces an exact duplicate of any document. However, the new product didn't have the market demand anticipated and only produced $35M in revenues in 1986, and for all of Federal Express revenues were $2.6B. Operating losses between 1985 and 1986 for ZapMail was $254M. Then in 1986, the company refocused back on its core competency of courier delivery services and in 2017 is earning revenue in excess of $319B.[8]

Company: Energy Resource Distributor

The Success Story: A Turkish energy resource distributor, has been using the Balanced Scorecard as a method to create a strategic focus. With the success of this approach over a 10-year period, gas volume increased 10x, subscribers 4x, customer satisfaction went up to 90%, and net profits almost tripled.

Company: Asian Power Company

The Success Story: 2008 was the beginning of an economic crisis and the first large deficit for this large power company. Afterwards the company adopted a strategic focused approach to clarify its vision, objectives and develop a viable long-term business strategy. In one year, the company went from a 2008 deficit of 139.5 billion to a 2009 profit of 211.6 billion and became number one among their five thermal power companies in the nation.

Company: Blue Apron

The Setback: Blue Apron reported disappointing earnings results in August 2017 due to difficulties ramping up a new, highly automated fulfillment center. The slow ramp up resulted in layoffs, an increase in order mistakes, late deliveries, and ultimately lowering customer retention rates. With customer retention rates already going down, marketing dollars to bring in new customers was reduced.[7]

Company: Starbucks

The Success Story: In 1971, Starbucks took up residence in Seattle's historic Pike Place Market and was serving free samples within 30 days. Today this company has more than 11,000 stores across the United States and $15 billion in annual revenue. What's even more impressive is that when you walk into any Starbucks, you are going to get the same customer experience whether you are in Indianapolis, IN or Stratford-upon-Avon in England.[6]

Strategic Focus: What's the Diagnosis?

How do you know if strategic focus is lacking? Well, it's painful for everyone and usually difficult to pinpoint the cause.

It's very common for organizations to want to do everything. And if it doesn't cost any hard dollars, you may put a little bit of your time towards a little bit of everything. Working a little bit on something makes a person feel like they are working towards a goal and are productive. However, feeling personally productive and being actually productive for the business are two very different things.

Unfortunately, this situation isn't unique. I have experienced it at most companies, and I hear similar stories from my peers regarding where they have worked. Having a lack of strategic focus was the root cause of many other symptoms they were experiencing, including:

- Employees are not showing up for meetings because they had another conflicting meeting for a project that was just as important;
- Employees burned out and high turn-over because they were trying to juggle too much work;
- Performing duplicative work on similar projects;
- Not able to spend approved capital funding which meant the organization might not receive funding for following years;
- Missed deadlines;
- Quality issues due to short-cuts just to meet a deadline.

There were multiple contributing factors to the lack of strategic focus, including:

1. Lack of an aligned set of objectives to achieve the vision;
2. No resource planning for all the projects, as well as the on-going business across the organization;
3. Leaders not collaborating;
4. Lack of prioritization;
5. Lack of quality project planning;

6. Lack of project selection to ensure the work is aligned and is the right work to do;
7. Lack of visibility into project needs including resources, costs, schedules, milestones, deliverables, risks, etc.
8. Lack of setting expectations;

While fixing the problem always seems daunting, you must get started. Even the smallest steps go a long way.

Looking back at many companies, it's somewhat surprising that most of them were good at establishing a vision and a mission. A few of them had documented and displayed their values daily. These were proudly featured on the website, business cards, all key marketing materials, and the employee handbook. However, that's where it ended. The vision wasn't broken down so that each employee knew exactly how they played a part in achieving that vision. Employees were not accountable for the values. And the mission statements were so long; no one could repeat it or knew the true meaning.

However, one company, Palentine, knew exactly how to take their vision and break it down. They had strategic initiatives. The company and each department had their vision, strategy, scorecard, metrics, targets, and initiatives that aligned with the company. Then each employee's performance was aligned with their department. The vision, mission, and values were simple, and every employee can repeat them without fail. On top all of that, every initiative was prioritized, and the entire company monitored its progress and reviewed it quarterly. Palentine was operating at a strong Level 5 for Strategic Focus.

The Assessment:

There are a few questions to ask yourself to identify what you need to get the strategic focus capability back on track.

1. Do you have a vision, mission, targets, and a strategy to execute? Is it up to date? Does everyone else in your organization know what it is and can articulate it?
2. Are you aware of market opportunities and conscientiously decide to go after them quickly? Are these opportunities aligned with your strategy?

3. Is your organization's performance aligned with the execution of number 1 (above)?
4. Do you track the execution?
5. What percentage of your strategic execution is effective; is it at least 80%? Do you challenge it?
6. Do you have a budget aligned to execute the strategy? Is the budget sufficient to succeed?
7. Have you prioritized the execution of your strategy and is there anything competing with the rest of the execution?
8. Do you have the talent (capacity, skills, and knowledge) to execute the strategy?

Baseline Your Maturity Level:

Level 1: Reactive Management:

You can't answer "Yes" to any of the questions above. Or, you can't answer yes to #1, 4, 6, and 7. Everything seems a bit unpredictable and reactive.

Level 2: Inconsistent Management:

You can answer "Yes" to #1, 4, 6, and 7.

Level 3: Defined:

You can answer "Yes" to #1, 4, 6, 7, and 8.

Level 4: Capability Quantitatively Managed:

You can answer "Yes" to #1, 3, 4, 6, 7, and 8.

Level 5: Optimizing Change Management:

You can answer "Yes" to every question.

Your baseline maturity level for Strategic Focus is: _____

Strategic Focus: Mind the Gap

Success in your organization is all about how well you manage your strategy. It's hard to accomplish anything without knowing where you're going and have everyone ready to go with you. There are hundreds of things you and your organization could spend your time on, but the entire intent of having strategic focus is to "focus" on what you are good at doing, doing it well, and not wasting any time doing anything else.

After diagnosing your Strategic Focus maturity, the next steps are as follows:

Level 1: Reactive Management:

1. Understand where you really are, do a SWOT (strengths, weaknesses, opportunities, and threats) for your business. Be honest.
2. Do a competitive landscape analysis and evaluate the market opportunities. Are they aligned with your core competencies?
3. Understand what capabilities are key to your success (use this book) and rate yourself on these capabilities.
4. Understand where you want to be in two to five years. Don't go too far out.
5. Create an inspiring vision and mission.
6. Identify the metrics you are going to use to track progress (leading and lagging).
7. Set yearly targets to achieve the vision.
8. Select the values of your organization (see the chapter on Values).
9. Identify how you are going to achieve the vision, break down the vision into more manageable objectives, and create targets for the objectives.
10. Assign an owner to each objective. Make sure the owner is accountable for success.
11. Establish a budget to achieve each objective.
12. Prioritize the work to accomplish the objectives.
13. Set a schedule to review this plan consistently.

Level 2: Inconsistent Management:

1. Estimate the hours (weekly, monthly, quarterly) required from the organization to accomplish the strategy to make sure the organization is not over-stretched.
2. Document the vision, mission, objectives, and targets and share with the organization.
3. Share the priorities and the plan to accomplish the work.

Level 3: Defined:

1. Baseline the metrics you established for the vision and the objectives above.
2. Break down the targets into quarterly targets.
3. Revisit everything to ensure it is achievable yet stretches the organization both in time, money and value to the organization.

Level 4: Capability Quantitatively Managed:

1. You have reviewed the organization's strategy above at least twice within the year.
2. Cascade the work through the organization. Have business units run through the steps above for their areas.
3. Align individual performance plans to the strategy.
4. Business units have reviewed their strategy at least twice.

Level 5: Optimizing Change Management:

1. Make adjustment decisions to the plan during strategy reviews based on progress.
2. Consistently review new market opportunities and discuss any changes to your plan.
3. Know how successful the entire strategy is and share it transparently with the organization.

Chapter 4

Leadership

"The competitive advantage of any company comes from excellent execution. The execution of strategy is driven by the behavior of leaders." - Maarten Hulshoff, former CEO, Rodamco Europe N.V.

"Insecure Leaders NEVER develop people. They replace them." - John Maxwell, American speaker, author, and pastor

The Vision:

We excel at building and inserting leaders throughout the organization with behaviors that inspire, motivate, and drive a positive impact on the organization to effectively execute our strategy.

What the Data Says:

- 30% of Fortune 500 company CEOs last fewer than three years.[1]
- Leadership development is a top priority for organizations. However, 36% do not have a formal leadership development strategy. Also, 77% of organizations do not have effective alignment between their leadership strategy and business strategy.[2]
- Only 28% of Millennials think their current employer makes full use of their skills.[3]
- Emotional intelligence is a key leadership differentiator—the ability to understand your effect on others and manage yourself accordingly—accounts for nearly 90% of career growth.[4]
- Executives who lacked emotional intelligence were rarely rated "outstanding" in their annual performance reviews, and their divisions underperformed by an average of almost 20%.[5]
- 86% of business and HR leaders believe they do not have an adequate leadership pipeline with only 38% see it as an urgent problem.[6]
- 75% of American employees report that their direct line manager is the worst part of their job, and 65% would take a pay cut if they could replace their boss with someone better.[7]
- A recent McKinsey report suggests that fewer than 30% of organizations can find the right C-suite leaders.[7]

The Meaning:

The continuity and effectiveness of our leadership experienced by employees have a significant impact on the organization's stakeholders, particularly customers, and ultimately our bottom line. Consistent leadership behaviors, values, and expectations experienced by employees lead to clarity about what is truly important. Clarity and effectiveness of our leaders positions employees to respond to and deliver what customers need. Companies that consistently produce effective leaders have a very clear leadership philosophy. The expectations are well understood on what leaders should know, how they should behave, and for what they are accountable. In the for-profit world, these organizations' leaders are easily distinguished from their competitors' or in non-profits, are clearly seen as community leaders that serve the greater good. When you choose to excel at leadership, it will be the driving force that leads to the success of many other capabilities. This capability also works in concert with domain expertise and innovation to drive your organization into the success of new markets and sustain it, ultimately bringing the long-term organizational value.

Examples:

Below are a few company examples of setbacks, success stories, and turnarounds where Leadership was mature or missing.

Company: Amazon.com

The Inspiring: Per Fortune's 2017 World's Greatest Leaders, Jeff Bezos ranks #5. Bezos has already disrupted the retail industry with Amazon.com that went online in 1995, surpassing Walmart in 2015 as the most valuable retailer in the United States. Amazon.com accounted for 43% of online sales in the U.S. in 2016.[8]

Bezos, with a net worth beyond anything most can imagine and is now one of the richest men in the world, displays remarkable leadership traits and a focus on organizational capabilities that have led to his success over the years. First and foremost, with his leadership traits, he consistently displays humility, inspiration, and effective communication. Through the success of his company, you can see Customer Service, Innovation, Continuous Learning, and Strategic Focus are at the top of the capabilities where Amazon excels.

Company: Borders

The Setback: Borders went completely out of business in 2011, with a huge part of that likely came at the hands of its biggest competitor: Amazon.com. Borders made a decision back in 2000 to partner with Amazon to control all of its online book sales. If the leader who made that decision purchased stock in Amazon back then (approximately $89/share), they would be very profitable with today's share price (approximately $1290/share).

Company: Circuit City

The Setback: Do you remember Circuit City? A huge part of their downturn started back in 2000 trying to cut costs. They found it very difficult to compete with Best Buy when the company decided to stop selling appliances; a very stable market with long-term demand. Instead, the company decided to focus solely on consumer electronics such as TVs and cameras. Then in 2003 they stopped paying commissions to their sales force and laid off their most experienced salespeople. Circuit City closed its doors in 2009.

Leadership: What's the Diagnosis?

How do you know if leadership is lacking in your organization? Can you quantify it? Can you qualify it? Do you use your gut? Do you assess people based on how you lead as to whether or not your organization not led well? Are you paying attention or is your focus elsewhere? Every organization requires different styles of leadership and different times of their growth. Whether you are a non-profit providing human services or a high-growth for-profit organization, the maturity of an organization and its various functions require different leadership styles. Establishing what you have and what you need is critical to your organization's mission and vision. The ultimate success of any organization's vision is defined by its top leadership. Their styles, the values they display, how well they influence, how they connect and communicate, if they have a vision, and so on, are just a small part of that definition and success.

While Palentine's Strategic Focus was operating at a Level 5, the company struggled with Leadership. One key leader was extremely intelligent, and the majority of the company reported up through him. His relationships and knowledge were acquired specifically to help to turn the company around. Where he truly struggled in his leadership, though, was that he had very few followers.

The most impactful experience was during a discussion during a conference call between myself, this leader, eight managers, and our service provider. During this conversation, the provider informed us that their shipment was going to be two months late. At this point, the leader took over the conversation and screamed into the phone, "If your company were on fire, I wouldn't even bother pissing on you to help put out the flames!" Total shock filled the room. The leader completely lost the respect of the room that day. After that call, this leader pulled me and one other into the same room and proceeded to jump up and down like a two-year-old throwing a tantrum, screaming about the situation. With the level of influence this leader had at the company, his impact would take years to overcome.

Leadership is one of the passionate topics I love to discuss, because of that, I really want to share another story.

At another company, one of our influential leaders, Bill, had a "weather report." Anytime someone would need to speak with this leader; they would head over to his assistant and ask, "What is the weather like today?" The hope was that it was a sunny day. If cloudy, you were taking a chance that your idea or news would fall on deaf ears, and on a stormy day, getting yelled at was normal behavior. If it was a stormy day and things could wait, meetings would normally get postponed. If it was a cloudy day, depending on how you were feeling, you might take a chance. If you are unpredictable in your leadership, how do you think that impacts your team and peers?

When assessing your leadership team, many identify various traits that they feel are important for their company to be successful. These could include strategic thinking, innovation, etc. Do also remember to assess based on common traits that employees want in a leader. You want a leader that others will follow.

When you look at the research in this area, you will come up with anywhere from two to twenty-two variations. I have summed up a shorter list of eight leadership traits for you to consider. These are not necessarily mutually exclusive:

1. Effective Communication: (See the chapter on this topic Effective Communication.)
2. Confidence: A leader will not only display confidence in themselves, but they show it regularly for everyone around them. They find the best in people. A leader who displays this well when things are going well, in addition, in times of stress and crisis, has a solid foundation of confidence.
3. Inspiring: The leader with this trait has passion and purpose for what they do, and it is contagious. They have a passion for their people and give their time and attention generously. They have a vision for the future and can inspire others to strive for that vision.
4. Optimistic: Optimism is contagious, and in times of crisis it is most critical to ensure employees can remain productive and think through difficult problems.
5. Decisive: Making quality and quick decisions for any leader is critical. We are faced with many each day. The act of making no decision is, in fact, making a decision. It just doesn't feel that way

for the leader's followers. Being decisive is an inspiring leadership trait that employees respect.
6. Authentic: This trait also encompasses other similar traits such as trust, honesty, integrity, accountability, and transparency. A leader needs to be trusted before they have a true following. People inside and outside a company need to feel they can trust a leader's words are genuine they are consistent with their behavior, and both their words and actions align. Personal accountability is strong.
7. Open Minded: A willingness to listen to others' thoughts and ideas and then to change when change is needed is critical for a leader.
8. Humility: Humility is about managing one's ego. Being realistic about situations and displaying a willingness to listen and learn, admit mistakes, and giving credit to those that deserve it. A strong display of humility says a lot about the self-confidence, self-awareness, and self-management of a leader.

The Assessment:

1. Baseline your leadership:

To determine whether or not you have the necessary leadership level for your organization, perform a simple assessment on the top two layers of your organizational structure. Do this by asking yourself and the employees the following questions:

People Leadership:

- What is your turnover rate? Does it seem high? What is the cause if it is?
- How is the employee morale or engagement in your organization?
- Is there healthy trust with your leadership? Does your leadership act with integrity?
- Is there healthy communication? Do your leaders practice a strong level of emotional intelligence?

- Is work taken seriously, but the people aren't taking themselves too seriously?
- Does your leadership recognize potential and reward performance?
- Does your leadership exhibit the values of your organization?
- Do your leadership actively show care for others?
- Does your leadership develop their employees or do they find it easier to fire them?

Leadership Performance:

- Does the leadership have a clear and achievable vision?
- Are they inspiring their teams with the vision?
- Does your leadership produce results?
- Are there clear priorities?
- Does your leadership practice accountability consistently?
- Does your leadership have the purpose and passion to drive the organization effectively, with the courage to challenge the status quo, and make quick and tough decisions? The courage to do the right things at the right time.

Customer Focus:

- Does your leadership have an outside-in mentality?
- Does your leadership know how to continuously improve and innovate, to exceed their customers' needs?
- Does your leadership have good relationships with their customers?
- Do they understand your short-term and long-term business needs?

Organizational Leadership:

- What type of organization do you have and what leadership is required? For example, if you are a non-profit organization serving people, you may find you need (per the DiSC behavioral assessment) an "agent" pattern style for key parts

in your organization as a whole that supports, harmonizes, empathizes, and focuses on service. However, you may need a leadership style that supports this type of organization well. Such as a coaching type of leader who develops people for the future, or a democratic leader who needs to build consensus in the organization. Or perhaps it's a combination?
- Do you have depth in leadership with people ready to step into the role?

2. Determine where, target levels, and timing to make a change:

Now that you know where your leadership level is, determine if this is the level you desire. Does each functional/service leader possess the type of leadership your organization should have?

Identify for each function/service where the type of leadership that's required is critical. For example, if your primary business required excellent customer service, does your leadership drive the high customer service results you expect? What are the key leadership traits this function requires? How deep is the leadership bench for the function/service?

3. Identify options for improvements:

What tools/programs/training do you have in place to acquire or build and continue to grow your leadership? What do you need in place?

Example Scenario:

1. Baseline your leadership:

An example value stream for a software product organization is as follows:

Marketing > Sales > Implementation > Customer Service

The critical functions with this example include implementation and customer service to ensure high quality and quick implementation. The leadership in each of these areas is critical to the overall revenue flow of the organization.

During the baseline phase of the assessment, you determine that the people leadership assessment in the implementation function have a very low score. Turnover is high, and employee morale is low. There is no vision for the function, and there are ten #1 priorities. Furthermore, the other functions in the organization don't like working with the top leader of the implementation function.

The leader of this organization has a coercive style that demands immediate compliance. They are very effective in crisis mode, but that is not how you want your organization to operate consistently.

2. Determine the areas of the organization, what target levels, and timing to make a change:

You then determine that the implementation of your product is the lifeblood of the organization. If you have no product, then you have no sales or need for customer service. Therefore, having leadership in this area of your business is the top priority. Next, you make the decision you need a combination of a coach and democratic leader so they can both develop people for the future of your organization while creating buy-in inside their organization and across the organization.

3. Options for improvements:

Based on the rate of turnover and the forecast on revenue, change in the leadership needs to be immediate. There's no time to train and coach the existing leader, so the search is on. A good relationship with a recruiting firm is the best option.

Baseline Your Maturity Level:

Rank your organization's leadership maturity for each function based on the levels below and then rolled up into one overall score.

Level 1: Capable Individual, but Inconsistent Management:

This leader makes productive contributions through their own, personal talent. This type of leader will do the work themselves with little delegation or collaboration. They make all the decisions and share very little information.

Turnover is likely high, employee morale is low, using all expertise to fight fires is the norm.

Level 2: Contributing Individual performing People Management:

This leader will contribute to team objectives and collaborates well with others. There is still little delegation, management of people, coaching, or mentoring within their organization. They have a team of self-directed individuals.

Performance objectives are unclear, and there is a lack of feedback. Employee morale is low, and turnover exists on average, but it feels very painful when someone leaves.

Level 3: Competent Manager performing Competency Management:

This leader is capable of organizing people to achieve objectives. The behaviors, skills, goals, and objectives for the critical functions are well understood and documented. Career opportunities are clear, and employee morale is average. Knowledge is openly shared. Metrics are in place to measure performance.

Level 4: Effective Leader Performing Capability Management:

An Effective leader operates as a catalyst, creating commitment with a clear vision. Their team is engaged and has high performance. Succession planning is in place. Employee morale is good, and turnover is low. Little fire-fighting exists. Individuals feel empowered to perform their role. Metrics are in place to predictably measure productivity, bench, morale, and organizational risk. Productivity is Level 3 or higher.

Level 5: Leadership Optimizing Change Management:

An Optimizing Leader builds enduring greatness throughout the entire organization through their capability to transform an organization and is proactively prepared for change. The entire organization has a passion for continuous improvement. Mentors and coaches exist in the organization, providing improvements for both individuals and teams. Competencies and capabilities are continuously improved. Productivity is operating at higher levels of maturity.

Your baseline maturity level for Leadership is: _____

Leadership: Mind the Gap

With Leadership, it's all about how much of it you have and the results your leadership can produce.

After diagnosing where you are with Leadership, you're ready for the next steps. No matter what your leadership baseline level is, these are the key talent strategy tactics to employ:

Level 1 through Level 5:

1. Create a Leadership Strategy based on your corporate strategy needs with the leadership style and quality necessary to execute your strategy.
2. Identify the key leadership traits you value in your organization.
3. Perform leadership style assessments. For example, the DiSC, SAOL Leadership Diagnostic, the Birkman, and the Maxwell Leadership Assessment are great tools.
4. Identify the leadership potential, including the capable individuals you already have in the leadership roles and others you already have in the organization. Understand their gaps based on the assessments and key leadership traits.
5. Perform a strategic talent review with the data captured above, starting with the top two layers of leadership. This review can be done yearly to quarterly.
6. Create and execute development plans. Depending on the level of the leader and their needs, development plans could be as simple as basic leadership training on emotional intelligence, speaking opportunities, group leadership, or as comprehensive as performing another role in the organization to enhance their knowledge and getting their MBA.
7. Execute effective performance management practices.
8. Establish succession planning and create a leadership forecast for the next two years.
9. Collect key metrics for performance, potential, employee morale, development plan execution, productivity, bench strength, recruiting pipeline, and organizational risk.

10. Develop relationships with executive coaches to help hold you and your leaders accountable.
11. Display caring. When you care about your employees, they tend to work harder and aim to exceed your expectations. Employees want to follow those who genuinely care about who they are and what they represent to the team and organization. Don't just view your employees as tools resources for your success, but as people and valuable assets who bring unique capabilities beyond their job functions. Employees want leaders who care about their general well-being and who can be dependable upon during times of professional and personal hardships.
12. At least yearly, review your leadership maturity level.

Chapter 5

Talent

> *"Women are the largest untapped reservoir of talent in the world."*
> *- Hillary Clinton, American politician and First Lady of the U.S.*

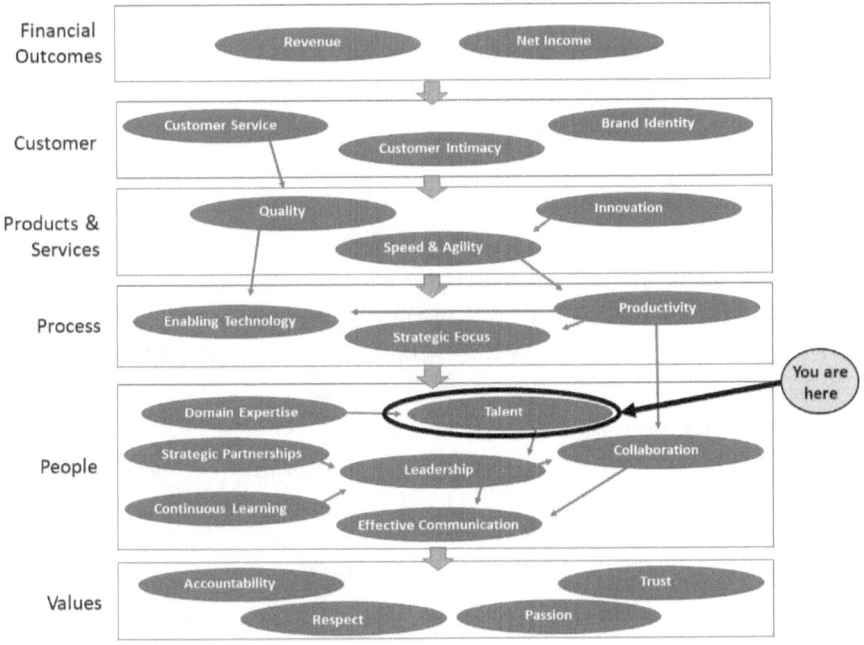

The Vision:

Leaders excel at attracting, developing, motivating, and retaining capable and dedicated people.

What the Data Says:

- The average cost of a bad hiring decision can equal 30% of the individual's first-year potential earnings.[1]

- As much as 80% of employee turnover is due to bad hiring decisions, and turnover costs 150% of the salary of the employee who must be replaced. For high-level or highly specialized employees, that figure jumps to 400%.[1]
- Companies with high-impact learning programs generated, on average, 3x higher profit growth than their peers.[1]
- Companies that invest $1,500 in training per employee see an average of 24% higher gross profit margins and 218% higher revenue per employee than companies who invest less.[1]
- Lost productivity due to new hire learning curves can cost from 1% to 2.5% of total business revenues.[1]
- Increasing employee engagement investments by 10% can increase profits by $2,400 per employee, per year.[1]
- Over an 11-year time frame, companies that had a performance management culture grew net income by 756%, versus a 1% growth over the same period for those that did not.[1]
- Departments with managers who receive feedback on their strengths achieve 8.9% greater profitability.[1]
- CFOs spend at least 40% of their time on business performance management, but they estimate that 30% of their company's performance potential is lost due to ineffective performance management processes and behaviors.[1]
- Companies that implement regular employee feedback have turnover rates that are 14.9% lower than for employees who receive no feedback.[1]
- The potential gains of a strengths-based management approach are worth it. However, Gallup analysis reveals that people who use their strengths every day are 3x more likely to report having an excellent quality of life, 6x more likely to be engaged at work, 8% more productive and 15% less likely to quit their jobs.[2]
- 79% believe they have a significant retention and engagement problem (26% see it as urgent).[3]
- 77% do not feel they have the right HR skills to address the issue (25% urgent).[3]
- 75% are struggling to attract and recruit the top people they need (24% urgent).[3]

- Only 17% feel they have a compelling and engaging employment brand.[3]
- 26% of the US workforce is going to change jobs this year, and these are typically the most highly skilled and motivated people.[3]

The Meaning:

Dedicated employees have the skills for today's and tomorrow's business needs. These employees are willing to continuously leverage and build upon those skills on a regular and predictable basis and are willing to give discretionary effort towards the organization's goals. This capability excels as leaders learn the how to attract new talent, developing existing talent, acting on poor performers, and continuously motivating existing talent for a sustainable team.

Examples:

Below are a few company examples of setbacks, success stories, and turnarounds where Talent was mature or missing.

Company: Amazon.com

The Success Story: Jeff Bezos' displays leadership skills of innovator, visionary, and has a strategic focus on a culture of customer service and well-established core competencies. Bezos has led Amazon to be the largest Internet-based retailer in the world based on total sales and market capitalization. In 2015, Amazon surpassed Walmart as the most valuable retailer in the United States by market capitalization.

Company: A Bank

The Success Story: A public bank located in Chile provided financial services to consumers and companies. The bank launched a program that aligned employees, strategy, and mission, so all employees felt a greater connection to the organization. Employee engagement increased more than 50% within a four year period.

Company: Intel

The Inspiring: Brian Krzanich made headlines several times in 2015 for his move to focus on Intel's talent and diversify the staff of over 100,000 worldwide employees.

January 2015 (stock price approximately $36 in 2015 and $44.50 in 2017), Krzanich announced a $300 million, five-year plan to bring the company's workforce to "full representation" by 2020. "It's time to step up and do more," Krzanich said. "It's not just good enough to say we value diversity, and then have our workplaces and our industry not reflect the full availability and talent pool of women and underrepresented minorities."

What this act of leadership displays is a focus and value on their talent capability that will pay dividends long-term. From the outside looking in, you can also see the company is continuously learning and innovating.

Talent: What's the Diagnosis?

Symptoms:

How do you know if your organization's talent is lacking? This area is very similar to Domain Expertise. The primary difference is talent runs broadly and will focus on the skills and abilities within their function. Domain expertise focuses on the key thought leadership required for wide knowledge of the business domain of your business and the products and services you provide.

At Baltic, I remember feeling so proud of the team I helped build. Strong leaders, knowledgeable, continuously learning, respecting each other, accountable to each other. They would anticipate my questions and raise issues and risks. They knew when they could do better and would then do it.

The day I decided to leave that organization, while sad, I was also so proud of them. It was the first time I said with strong confidence to them, "I have done what I set out to do. You don't need me anymore. You are a self-led team achieving great things."

Now mind you, I have made some mistakes in selecting talent. The worse thing I could have ever done was rush to make a hiring decision and not listen to both my head and my intuition.

At Baltic, we had a major situation with a key domain expert and leader that decided to quit. Joe was very good, and it would be hard to lose him. At the same time, I would not miss his attitude. Joe helped me interview at least ten different candidates, but none with whom I really connected. I was in a position where I felt I needed to quickly hire Joe's backfill and he had highly recommended one of the ten we interviewed. Despite what my gut told me, we hired Carl.

Fast forward seven months, my phone would be ringing almost daily with complaints about Carl's attitude and how he was treating our clients. When I spoke with him about the situation on multiple occasions, all the finger pointing went in every direction except his own. Somehow it was the client's fault; it was the sales guy fault; it was my fault, and so on. My lesson: Never shortcut finding good talent.

The Assessment:

1. Identify for each function or service: What are the key skills and abilities required to perform successfully? Is there a gap in what is required vs. what you have?
2. Evaluate history for each function or service: Look back on the process speed, quality, and total output. Is it as expected? Is it above average or is it below average? What is the turnover?
3. Root cause analysis: Based on the primary value stream where critical talent is required, do you have any functions operating below average where the root cause is due to a lack of capacity or skills?

Baseline Your Maturity Level:

Level 1: Inconsistent Management (or "I don't know what I have"):

In each function or service, the required skills and abilities have not been identified. Turnover is likely high, morale is low, and pulling all expertise together to fight fires is the norm. Ramp up time isn't quantified.

Level 2: People Management:

You know the skills and abilities required, but there's a lack of knowledge. Performance objectives are unclear, and there is not enough feedback. Morale is low, and turnover exists on average, but it's painful when someone leaves because ramp up time is six months or more. Ramping up a new person involves one-on-one with other individuals.

Level 3: Competency Management:

The behaviors, skills, goals, and objectives for the function or service are documented. Career opportunities are clear, and employee morale is average. Knowledge is shared. Metrics are in place to measure performance.

Level 4: Capability Management:

Succession planning is in place, and the bench for critical talent is two levels deep. Employee morale is good, and turnover is low. If an individual does leave the organization, knowledge is transferred quickly, and firefighting does not exist. Individuals feel empowered to perform their role. Metrics are in place to predictably measure productivity, bench, morale, and organizational risk. Productivity is mid-level.

Level 5: Optimizing Change Management:

The entire organization is focused on continuous improvement with individuals. Mentors and coaches exist in the organization, providing improvements for both individuals and teams. Competencies and capabilities are continuously improved. Productivity is operating at high maturity levels.

Your baseline maturity level for Talent is: _____

Talent: Mind the Gap

With Talent, it's all about how much of it you have and how productive it is.

After diagnosing where you are in your function or service, the next steps are as follows:

Level 1: Inconsistent Management:

Stop the bleeding. This level is the most comprehensive. Give it your full attention.

1. Prioritize the functions or services and roles where talent is lacking.
2. Create the job descriptions and start recruiting.
3. Create the on-boarding and training documentation required to ramp up quickly.
4. Create a team of mentors to help new individuals ramp up.
5. Hire selectively.
6. Identify reasons for low employee morale.
7. Remove leadership problems (see the chapter on Leadership).

Level 2: Performance Management:

1. Get performance management processes and technology under control.
2. Train leaders on expectations for managing people well.
3. Promote information sharing.
4. Measure turnover.
5. Higher leadership coaches and train leadership mentors.

Level 3: Competency Management:

1. Document the behaviors, skills, goals, and objectives.
2. Create clear career growth opportunities.
3. Functional knowledge of roles is shared.
4. Metrics on performance are reviewed, and confidence in the data is high.
5. Put a learning management system in place.

Level 4: Capability Management:

1. Create succession plans for critical roles/knowledge.
2. Measure bench strength monthly.
3. Measure yearly and manage morale continuously.
4. Measure the rate of time that an employee is 100% productive in their role.
5. Ensure the organizational risk in each of the critical areas is low.
6. Review the rate that proactive activities are higher than reactive activities.
7. Develop functional specific mentors and coaches.
8. Forecast your needs for the next three to five years.

Level 5: Optimizing Change Management:

1. Measure the impact of learning in the organization.
2. Ensure increases in productivity have occurred.
3. Continuously improve all processes, competencies, knowledge, etc. from earlier levels.

Chapter 6

Domain Expertise

"True intuitive expertise is learned from prolonged experience with good feedback on mistakes." - Daniel Kahneman, Author, Psychologist, and Nobel Memorial Prize winner

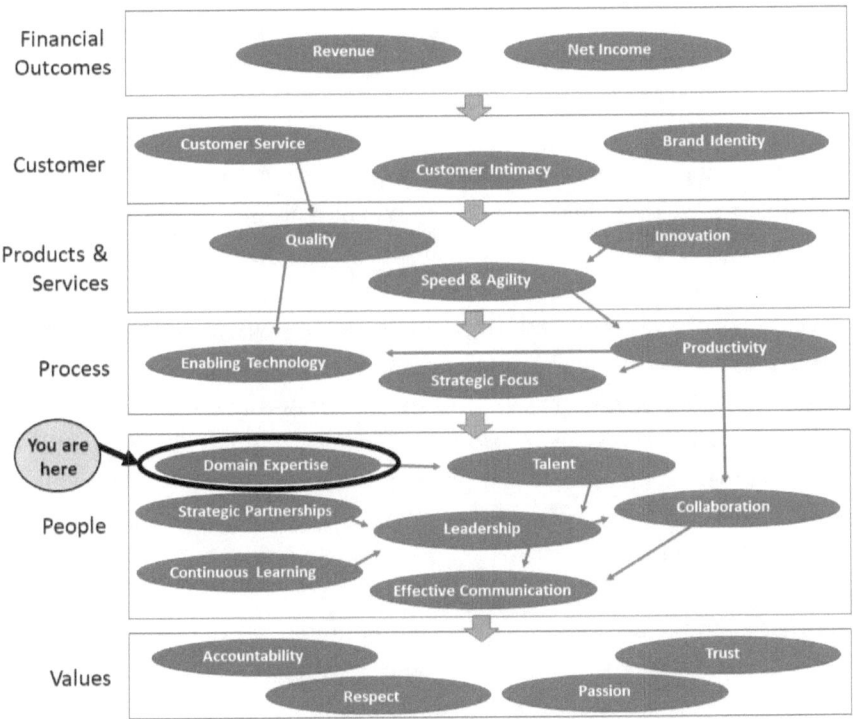

The Vision:

We have deep domain expertise that excels and clearly demonstrates thought leadership in the industry we serve and the products and services we provide.

What the Data Says:

- Product failure rate is estimated at 85% for consumer goods.[2]
- 30.3% of companies fail due to the lack of good business education for company management.[3]

The Meaning:

The wording of this organizational capability could also be in the form of business acumen, subject matter expertise, etc. The premise is the demonstration of specific talent or expertise in the industry you serve. It is the foundation of the success of the products and services you sell. For example, the industry knowledge involved in oil drilling; the development of mobile technology; or perfecting the location for a new CVS.

Domain experts must have a deep and wide knowledge of the business domain to provide value back to the business to make short- and long-term decisions. Domain experts will also have vertical market expertise such as healthcare where they understand how the customer uses their products specific to their industry. These experts will also have customer segment expertise such as hospitals and doctor offices within the healthcare industry. A domain expert will also have a cross-market expert with the ability to infer similarities in product offerings, regulatory needs, and to follow an overall lifecycle to the products offered—for example, a billing product that can be utilized by customers in vertical markets of hospitals, banking, and car sales.

Another example of domain expertise is an understanding of the lifecycle of how various types of debt is collected with an accounts receivables product, such as hospital bills, credit card debt, and car loans, as well as a knowledge of where these markets are heading in the future.

Depending on the type of product you sell, your customers may also drive substantial wealth from both the knowledge and the use of the products you sell. Making this capability essential to your business.

Excelling in this capability will position a company to be seen as a thought leader and trusted advisor in their industry. Without this, brand identity can diminish and deplete overall brand equity. This capability has a strong correlation with driving innovation to continuously create the needs of your market. Once lost, the underlying foundational power that domain expertise provides to other capabilities is extremely difficult to regain quickly.

Examples:

Below is a company example of a setback where Domain Expertise was missing.

Company: Palentine

The Setback: At Palentine, when the leaders downsized a large portion of the company, they didn't anticipate the impact of the domain expertise that would be lost. This loss included customer service agents to troubleshoot product problems, employees that knew how to implement the product, sales people with expertise in selling across all their markets, and employees that knew how to make product changes effectively. The total amount of wages saved paled in comparison to the overall loss of customers and millions of dollars in revenue.

It's also possible for too much of the same domain expertise, or a surplus of intelligence, to be a detriment to a company. What if your company hired only the same gender of engineers? See Liz Wiseman - Multipliers and Rookie Smarts.[1] When you know nothing, it puts you in a position to ask questions and explore ideas. When you have too much "like-thinking," or you are constantly tapping into the same experiences, you will feel you have the answer and repeat activities the same way without exploring new ideas. Innovation may not occur, and diversity of thought will be lacking. When we know the pattern and the information, we often stop innovating, and this creates blind spots. It's very similar to driving home down the same road every day. You operate on autopilot. Sometimes, you even forget the drive home. You might even miss new scenery along the way or accidentally hit a new pothole because you weren't looking for it. This state of thinking is called unconscious competence.

Experience provides lessons learned with both positive experiences and scars—distant memories that remind you of successes and the mistakes you've made. If you are the one with new ideas, you may touch on someone else's scar tissues. And if they are risk averse, they may even admonish your new ideas. Ignorance, or unconscious incompetence, will start you in a place where you don't know how hard something can be. Then, after some time, you move into awareness, conscious incompetence, on how hard something is. For some, this is an uncomfortable place, and we are in a position where there's no other choice but to learn. Next, desperation kicks in because we want to avoid new scars. Learning then becomes exponential, and this when a person will experience conscious competence.

Domain Expertise: What's the Diagnosis?

Symptoms:

How do you know if domain expertise is lacking in places where it is most critical, especially if you don't have the metrics in place? Typically, this would be a leading indicator when assessing your people. There are a few questions to ask yourself to identify if this capability is required or lacking.

As mentioned earlier, Palentine experienced a downsizing of a large number of people. Inside of this number existed domain experts for their products, the lifeblood of the company. Knowledge of how it was built, how it was to be implemented, how to train people, and how it worked all walked out the door. The company truly suffered and spent more on the bottom line overall to recover. It took longer to, fix the problem and customers eventually became upset and left.

The Assessment:

1. Identify critical functions: What are the key functions where domain expertise for your business' primary value stream is critical, important, and nice to have. If you are a company like Amazon, customer experience experts may be considered critical. Or, if you are a Pharmaceutical company, experts may be found with your scientists.
2. Evaluate history of critical functions: Look back on the process speed, quality, and total output. Is it as expected? Is it above average? Or is it below average? What is the turnover experienced?
3. Root cause analysis: Based on the primary value stream where critical domain expertise is required, do you have any functions operating below average?

Example Scenario:

1. Identify critical functions:

The value stream for an example software product company is as follows:

Marketing > Sales > Implementation > Customer Service

The critical functions with this example include Implementation and Customer Service to ensure high quality and quick implementation. The domain expertise includes expert knowledge of the customer's business industry and the software product itself. Sales is an important part of the value stream, but not critical, while marketing is nice to have as the function-focused primarily on trade shows and one-on-one interaction.

2. Evaluate history of critical functions:

Implementation has taken two years in the past, while nine months is the target. This lag is causing a backup of potential revenue.

3. Root cause analysis:

Root cause analysis shows that domain expertise is thin and will take extreme efforts to increase quickly, based on the number of simultaneous implementations. While there has not been a loss of domain expertise within the implementation team, the number of implementations building up is putting additional stress on the existing staff. This situation poses a risk of staff leaving if a remedy is not identified.

In addition to the customer service area, customer satisfaction scores have been averaging about 2.5 on a scale of 5. That means if customers could easily change companies, many of them would have already done so.

Baseline Your Maturity Level:

Level 1: Inconsistent Management (or "I don't know what I have"):

In the areas of your critical functions, domain expertise has not been identified. Turnover is likely consistent, employee morale is low, pulling all expertise together to fight fires is the norm, and ramp-up time isn't quantified.

Level 2: People Management:

You know the level of expertise for each of the critical functions, but there's a lack of knowledge in the critical functions. Performance objectives are unclear, and there is a lack of feedback. Employee morale is low, and turnover exists on average, but it's painful when someone leaves since ramp-up time is six months or more. Ramping up a new person usually involves one-on-one with other individuals who are already over capacity.

Level 3: Competency Management:

The behaviors, skills, goals, and objectives for the critical functions are documented. Career opportunities are clear, and employee morale is average. Knowledge is shared. Metrics are in place to measure performance.

Level 4: Capability Quantitatively Management:

Succession planning is in place, and the bench for domain expertise is two levels deep. Employee morale is good, and turnover is low. If an individual does leave the organization, knowledge is transferred quickly, and firefighting is virtually non-existent. Individuals feel empowered to perform their role. Metrics are in place to predictably measure productivity, bench, employee morale, and organizational risk. Productivity is Level 3 or higher.

Level 5: Optimizing Change Management:

The entire organization is focused on continuous improvement with individuals. Mentors and coaches exist in the organization, providing improvements for both individuals and teams. Competencies and capabilities are continuously improved. Productivity is at Level 4 or 5.

Your baseline maturity level for Domain Expertise is: _____

Domain Expertise: Mind the Gap

With Domain Expertise, it's all about how much of it you have and how effectively it is leveraged in the critical areas you need.

After diagnosing where you are with Domain Expertise, the next steps are as follows:

Level 1: Inconsistent Management

Stop the bleeding. This level is the most comprehensive. Don't take any shortcuts.

1. Prioritize the critical functions and roles where Domain Expertise is lacking.
2. Create job descriptions and start recruiting, or identify people who have a great deal of domain expertise that could be better leveraged in higher, more critical areas.
3. Create on-boarding and training documentation required to ramp-up quickly for new or existing employees.
4. Create a team of mentors to help new individuals ramp up.
5. Hire selectively.
6. Identify reasons for low employee morale.
7. Remove leadership problems (see the chapter on <u>Leadership</u>).

Level 2: Performance Management:

1. Get performance management processes and technology under control.
2. Train leaders on expectations for managing people well.
3. Promote information sharing.
4. Measure turnover.
5. Higher leadership coaches and train leadership mentors.

Level 3: Competency Management:

1. Document the behaviors, skills, goals, and objectives.
2. Create clear career growth opportunities.

3. Functional knowledge of roles are documented and easily shared.
4. Metrics on performance are reviewed, and confidence in the data is high.
5. Put a learning management system in place.

Level 4: Capability Quantitatively Management:

1. Create succession plans for critical functions.
2. Measure bench strength monthly.
3. Measure the rate of time that your domain expertise is 100% productive in their role.
4. Ensure the organizational risk in each of the critical areas is low.
5. Review the rate that proactive activities are higher than reactive activities.
6. Develop domain expertise mentors and coaches.
7. Forecast your needs for a predetermined number of years.

Level 5: Optimizing Change Management:

1. Measure the impact of learning in the organization.
2. Increases in productivity have occurred.
3. Continuously improve all processes, competencies, and knowledge from earlier levels.

Chapter 7

Productivity

"Nothing is less productive than to make more efficient what should not be done at all." - Peter Drucker, author, educator, and management consultant

The Vision:

We effectively spend our dollars, time, and resources to be more productive and achieve our intended outcomes.

What the Data Says:

- Most employees want to be productive, but the organization too often gets in their way. Our research indicates that the average

company loses more than 20% of its productive capacity—more than a day each week—to what we call "organizational drag," the structures and processes that consume valuable time and prevent people from getting things done.[1]
- One inspired employee can produce as much as 2.25 satisfied employees.[1]

The Meaning:

Leaders who fail to manage costs through effective spending and balanced resource utilization will not likely have the same opportunities as those who do. You will need to acquire the talent and domain expertise necessary to innovate, maintain customer intimacy, and rapidly bring products to market that fund the overall growth of the top line. However, the effective spending of dollars is not enough. Having both a cost-efficient and a productive mindset is the next level of maturity for any organization. This type of organization removes obstacles and creates the ability for their workforce (this includes strategic partners, vendors, and consultants) to accomplish their work effectively. Companies use to have the mantra, "Do more with less," now there is a shift to, "Do more with the same." With higher labor productivity, a company can produce more goods and services with the same amount of relative work.

Examples:

Below are a few company examples of setbacks, success stories, and turnarounds where Productivity was mature or missing.

Company: Defense Information Services (IS) Department

The Success Story: The IS Department of this defense company transformed itself from a cost center to a strategic partner inside its parent company, consolidating numerous information technology systems and focusing on service with complete solutions. In doing so, the organization achieved 15% productivity savings with alignment to customer needs and elimination of ineffective work.

Additionally, the effective use of department products and services enabled internal customers to achieve 10% productivity savings.

Company: An Indonesia Pharmaceutical Company

The Success Story: A pharmaceutical company in Indonesia, was faced with increasing competition and escalating costs. To remain competitive, they transformed its operations and implemented process changes that improved total productivity. Production lead time was reduced from 25 days down to just two.

Productivity: What's the Diagnosis?

Symptoms:

Every organization inherently wants to be productive. It's an unspoken base expectation. Employees, more so, want to be productive, but "organizational drag" gets in the way. Decision-making, manual and duplicate efforts, and unnecessary work are just a few of the reasons processes may be slow. There are ways, however, to identify opportunities for improvement that make stakeholders, customers, senior leadership, and employees happy.

At Neolistics, productivity was a key issue. Research revealed that it took 18 pairs of hands from 10 departments more than 60 days to build just one server. With the use of agile techniques and focus, the group discovered that five days was achievable. It was amazing to see the potential for the amount of time, money, and even employee frustration that could be saved with improvements to the process.

The Assessment:

1. Identify for each function or service: Identify the key skills and abilities required to perform successfully. Is there a gap in what is required vs. what you have?
2. Evaluate history of each function or service:

    a. Do your processes meet or exceed expectations?
    b. Do you have the quality levels you expect?
    c. Does output meet or exceed expectations?
    d. Are processes streamlined without duplication?
    e. Are your customers satisfied with the output of your process?
    f. Are your processes documented and transparent to those who need access to the information?
    g. Do you train new employees on the processes?
    h. Are the costs associated with your processes scaled appropriately to perform?
    i. Are your processes as automated as they can be?
    j. Do your employees feel the processes are optimized?

k. Do you have metrics to track all of the above?
l. Do your employees have ideas on how to improve your processes that have been implemented over time?

Baseline Your Maturity Level:

Level 1: Initial:

You answered "No" to all questions above. Processes are unpredictable, poorly controlled, and reactive.

Level 2: Managed:

You answered "Yes" to some of 2a - 2f, but not all. Processes are defined for projects, but there's a lot of reactivity.

Level 3: Defined:

You answered "Yes" to 2a - 2f with fair confidence. Processes are documented for all business processes, and people are trained to perform them.

Level 4: Capability Quantitatively Managed:

You answered "Yes" to 2a - 2g with fair confidence. Processes are measured and controlled.

Level 5: Optimizing:

You answered "Yes" to all the questions. There's a focus on continuous process improvement.

Your baseline maturity level for Productivity is: _____

Productivity: Mind the Gap

After diagnosing where you are with your productivity levels, the next steps are as follows:

Level 1: Initial:

You answered "No" to all questions. Processes are unpredictable, poorly controlled, and reactive. Stop the bleeding. This level will be the most comprehensive step. Do not take shortcuts.

1. Prioritize the critical functions/key processes.
2. Document each key process in your value stream and test your documentation to ensure it is accurate.

Level 2: Managed:

You answered "Yes" to some of 2a - 2f, but not all. Processes are defined for projects, but there is much reactivity occurring.

1. Identify metrics for each key process in your value stream, both leading and lagging, how you will calculate each measure, and where the data will come from for the following areas:
    a. Quality
    b. Speed/Time
    c. Productivity
    d. Cost
    e. Customer satisfaction
    f. Automation

Level 3: Defined:

You answered "Yes" to 2a - 2f with fair confidence. Processes are documented for all business processes, and people are trained to perform them.

1. Document each key sub-process in your value stream and test your documentation to ensure it is accurate.
2. Train all staff on the processes.

Level 4: Capability Quantitatively Managed:

1. Create a dashboard with your key metrics from Level 3 (above). Review the metrics with team members using the processes and involving leadership.

Level 5: Optimizing:

1. Discuss opportunities for improvement with team members by evaluating causes for failures and improved success.
2. Prioritize the opportunities.
3. Continuously improve all processes, competencies, and knowledge from earlier levels.

Chapter 8

Continuous Learning

"Education is the kindling of a flame, not the filling of a vessel."
- Socrates, classical Greek philosopher

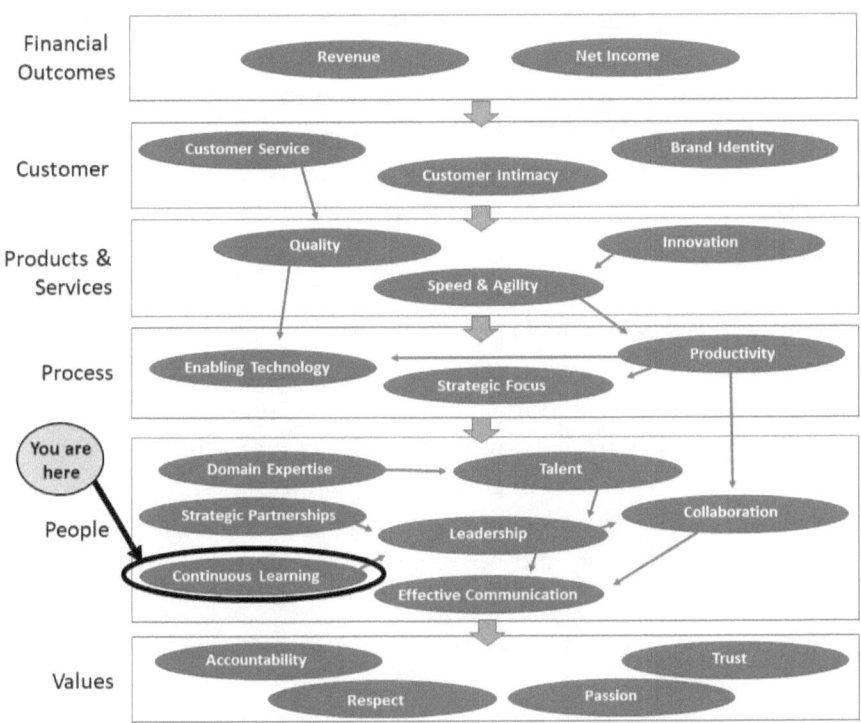

The Vision:

We're good at quickly acquiring new skills and knowledge, then disseminating them throughout the organization to improve what we know and do.

What the Data Says:

- There were 12.7 million unemployed Americans in 2010, while seven million skilled jobs went unfilled.[2]
- 93% of mid-level professional jobs require an Associates degree or higher, but only 38% of working age Americans have attained this level of education.[2]
- 94% of employers stated ongoing education is "important" for mid-level professionals, while 66% said it was "very important." Just-in-time learning is most critical for those in tech so that employees can stay up-to-date on ever-changing industry trends.[2]
- 70% of employers believe that employees need continuous learning simply to keep up with the demands of their current jobs.[2]
- 96% of employers agree that ongoing education has a positive impact on their employees' job performance.[2]

The Meaning:

Organizations generate new ideas and learn through training, research, experimentation, hiring new talent, and continuous improvement. This capability is leveraged at its highest potential for an organization when it gains the experience from learning and making use of that learning over time and can respond to change with speed and agility. For individuals, learning means we are open to discovering new things, including new ideas, ways of thinking, and opportunities to improve. As individuals collectively learn, their power is greater than any one individual.

Examples:

Below are a few company examples of setbacks, success stories, and turnarounds where Continuous Learning was mature or missing.

Company: AT&T

A Success Story: AT&T launched a program that combined online and classroom-based coursework in subjects like digital networking and data science that looks at old skills that can be transferred to new careers. It started this program in 2012. The demand for learning hasn't stopped, and based on the development life cycle of new digital technologies, which has sped up, the learning cycle will only get faster.[1]

Company: A Lynda.Com Customer

A Success Story: After customers noticed search engine optimization (SEO) results were down for a major product, the manager assigned an SEO training course to its product manager and traffic increased by 75% for their product searches.

Continuous Learning: What's the Diagnosis?

Symptoms:

Having a continuous learning environment is fundamental to building an innovative one. Expanding one's skills and knowledge benefits both for the individual (professionally) and the organization. Your company can fall behind in a blink if you don't provide your employees the opportunity to grow.

Many years ago, working in the technology division of a credit union, I first discovered the Rational Software suite. I had a passion for understanding how it worked because I saw the benefits it provided to software development teams. At the time, I was making a decent income for my age and schooling. I absorbed myself into learning to include all the ins and outs of how to use the software and administer it. Rational Suite made developing software that much easier. I discovered that having the skills as a subject matter expert with this software was in high demand. Indeed, my next two roles in the pharmaceutical industry proved to be profitable, increasing my income by $20K within three years.

As I continued to feed my desire to learn, I moved on from the Rational products and started learning about project management and gained my PMP (Project Management Professional) certification. This focus on learning earned me another raise and promotion, eventually leading to my move into consulting. At that point, I increased my income yet again by another $25K. Not too bad of an increase over 4.5 years. It required hundreds of hours of learning and a couple of hundred dollars for the cost of the certification test and two books, but it was well worth the investment.

I wasn't the only one who benefited though. With these new skills and the certification I gained, the company I worked for was able to bill me out at a higher rate, so we all profited in the end.

The Assessment:

1. Do you have any basic skills gaps in your organization?
2. Have you assessed the skills you have and the ones you need?
3. Do you provide mentoring and coaching in your environment?
4. Do you have a Learning Management System?
5. Does your leadership allow time to their employees for learning?
6. Do you provide incentives for employees to learn new skills and gain certifications?
7. Do you evaluate and receive the impact or outcomes of learning vs. the activity of learning? Do you get what you pay for regarding results from what your employees learn?
8. Do you have an organizational budget for learning?
9. Does your organization have a growth mindset?

Baseline Your Maturity Level:

Level 1: Non-learning Environment:

You can't confidently say "Yes" to any of the questions.

Level 2: Episodic Learning:

Some areas of the organization are learning, and you can say "Yes" to 1-2.

Level 3: Coordinated Learning:

You can confidently answer "Yes" to 1-4.

Level 4: Measured Learning:

You can answer "Yes" to 1-6.

Level 5: Continuous Learning Organization:

You can answer "Yes" to 1-8 annually with an increased budget each year.

Your baseline maturity level for Continuous Learning is: _____

Continuous Learning: Mind the Gap

On-going education is a critical reality, and the development of soft skills is the most important consideration for any business with an emphasis on required or technical skills.

After diagnosing where you are with your continuous learning levels, the next steps are as follows:

Level 1: Non-learning Environment:

1. Evaluate the key areas where learning is key, then select the top two.
2. Identify the skills required for the next three years in this area.
3. Assess the skill level of your current staff.
4. Determine the skills gap between today and what you need in three years.
5. Determine how you are going to close the gap in skills. Align these needs with business goals. Can you invest in who you have, and how will you do that? Or, do you need to buy the skills temporarily or permanently?
6. Formulate the development plan for the employees you are investing your time. Identify their training needed, methods for training, expected outcomes, and milestones.
7. Fund the development plans.

Level 2: Episodic Learning:

1. Execute the development plans for the top two areas.
2. Measure progress in the development plan.
3. Repeat level 1 for another few areas of your business.
4. Identify a Learning Management System to keep track of skills, gaps, development plans, and to administer training.
5. Build in mentoring and coaching programs.

Level 3: Coordinated Learning:

1. Execute your Learning Management System.
2. Repeat levels 1 and 2 for another few areas of your business.

Level 4: Measured Learning:

1. Evaluate the collective outcomes from the development plans. Are you getting the return on investment you expect?
2. Plan your budget for training and incentives for training by each department.

Level 5: Continuous Learning Organization:

1. Evaluate the progress of learning for the entire organization. Do 70% or more of your employees take advantage of learning?
2. Evaluate the skills gap. Have you identified the necessary skills for the entire organization?

Chapter 9

Innovation

"Innovation has nothing to do with how many R&D dollars you have. When Apple came up with the Mac, IBM was spending at least 100 times more on R&D. It's not about money. It's about the people you have, how you're led, and how much you get it." - Steve Jobs, American entrepreneur, co-founder, and CEO of Apple

The Vision:

We excel at generating ideas that drive an impact for our customers, employees, and organization.

What the Data Says:

- 5% of respondents report that workers in innovation programs feel highly motivated to innovate.[1]
- 81% say their firms do not have the resources needed to fully pursue the innovations and new ideas capable of keeping their companies ahead in the competitive global marketplace.[1]
- 49% believe they won't receive any benefit or recognition for developing successful ideas.[1]
- 83% of customers indicate that they would pay more for innovation in electronics.[3]
- 43% of business executives agreed that innovation is a "competitive necessity" for their organization.[3]

The Meaning:

Innovation with products, services, processes, and other capabilities, continuously have their sights on the future. Having a deep pipeline of innovative products and services is exciting for employees, customers, and builds confidence among shareholders. Companies who must excel in this capability will dominate and drive their existing markets and maintain long-term value for the organization.

For-profit companies exist to make money either for profit or to continue to provide services to their customers. For leaders who want to build a sustainable pipeline of innovation, ensure you are intentional about protecting your core competencies. Don't jeopardize those.

Examples:

Below are a few company examples of setbacks, success stories, and turnarounds where Innovation was mature or missing.

Company: Blackberry

The Setback: Do you remember the "CrackBerry?" It was the phone to have in the mid- to late-2000s. In 2007, it had more than half of the market share of phones in the U.S.

Also during this time in 2007; the iPhone was released. At first, Blackberry ignored touch screen-based technology, insisting their phones would remain the standard for enterprises, especially with the early iPhone struggles. Blackberry's initial inaction created a succession of failed attempts to innovate. Then by 2015, Blackberry held only 0.8% of the Smartphone market share.[2]

Company: Polaroid

The Setback: How many people have taken a Polaroid in the last ten years? Or, depending on your age, do you know what one looks like or what it is? Polaroid started out as an innovative brand that brought us instant photography. However, they didn't realize that digital cameras were going to be the wave of the future until it was way too late. Polaroid filed for bankruptcy in 2001 and film photography is now merely a niche market.

Company: Kodak

The Setback: Kodak had over 85 percent of the film and camera business by 1976, and their photofinishing process quickly became the industry standard for quality. But it will never be quite as powerful due to a huge mistake. Kodak invented digital photography in the 1970s, but company executives were too scared to move away from traditional film and didn't want to impact this part of their business. They also invented the VCR but didn't believe consumers would pay an estimated retail cost of $500. They even chose not to patent Xerox-like photocopying technology. Today, digital cameras and smartphones prevail. Kodak isn't dead, but it's nothing compared to what it once was.[2]

Company: InfoSys

The Success Story: InfoSys, an India based global IT service provider, leveraged a program to improve performance measures that increased innovation, measured by the percentage of revenue from new services, by 48%.

Company: Borders

The Setback: The 2011 bankruptcy of Borders symbolized the wider changes taking place in the book publishing industry. Borders failed to release an e-reader in a timely fashion. Amazon's Kindle came out in 2007, and Barnes & Noble released the Nook in 2009. Borders, on the other hand, waited until 2010 to release its Kobo—by then, it was too late.

Innovation: What's the Diagnosis?

Symptoms:

The speed required for new products and services to hit the market is exponential, putting a constant demand on any business to just maintain the current success, let alone go above and beyond. Here are a few ways to determine if innovation is a problem in your organization.

Innovation comes in so many forms. It can earn you extra revenue, save you on the bottom line, it can be small, and it can be big. One very simple innovation I did as a consultant comes to mind. The days-sales-outstanding (DSO, or how long it took for the company to get paid once the invoice was created) was well over 90 days. Using Six Sigma techniques to document the process we determined that the most problems existed in two places:

1. Once the invoice was printed, it was reviewed for accuracy. This process was taking on average more than two weeks.

2. The invoices were not always going to the right person or department at the client's location.

By speeding up the review cycle and ensuring we had the right contact for our client's accounts payable department, we decreased our DSO to less than 30 days. It was a small innovation, but one that resulted in significant cash flow impact for a small company that had more than $1M in accounts receivables in a given month.

The Assessment:

1. Do you have a pipeline of ideas in various stages of development?
2. Do you have sufficient funding and time to allow innovations to culminate?
3. Is your profit increasing annually?
4. Do you have a transparent and measurable innovation process?
5. Do you have an increasing profit forecast based on your innovation pipeline?

6. Does your leadership lead by example and embrace innovation? Meaning, do your leaders elicit and evaluate new ideas from their employees?
7. Does your organization have a focus on results vs. activity?
8. Do your innovations align with what you do well every day?
9. Are your innovations backed by a solid strategy? (Financial, competition, product management, sales, distribution, marketing, implementation, manufacturing, partners, suppliers, research, and development.)
10. Do you execute more innovative products and services better than your competition?
11. Are your people empowered and enabled to deliver innovation?

Baseline Your Maturity Level:

Level 1: Non-existent:

You cannot confidently answer "Yes" to any of the questions.

Level 2: Episodic Innovation:

You can answer "Yes" to number one because there are a few ideas in your innovation pipeline. Number two feels painful, but you do have some funding.

Level 3: Coordinated Innovation:

You feel confident answering "Yes" to questions 1-5.

Level 4: Innovative Leadership:

You can answer "Yes" to questions 1-8.

Level 5: Innovative Organization:

You can confidently answer "Yes" to all the questions.

Your baseline maturity level for Innovation is: _____

Innovation: Mind the Gap

The following is a very basic way to start creating an innovative culture. You may want to repeat this process a few times to get it going. There are more comprehensive programs listed in the "References and Other Related Resources" chapter.

Level 1: Non-existent:

1. Start educating the importance of innovation.
2. Assign an innovation executive sponsor to ensure accountability.
3. Dedicate a few people to generate and research new ideas.
4. Set aside money to get started. Consider increasing this after you reach Level 3 confidently.
5. Create company goals for generating ten good ideas you can research further and two you can immediately take to the market.

Level 2: Episodic Innovation:

1. Select a few ideas worth pushing further.
2. Ensure you have sufficient personnel and funding to take one idea to market.
3. Start reviewing what process you want to use to track your innovation pipeline. Make sure it's transparent and keep it simple.
4. Place goals on the performance plans of leaders/managers.

Level 3: Coordinated Innovation:

1. Implement your innovation process. Make sure you're still keeping it simple.
2. Educate everyone in the organization, so they know how to submit a new idea.
3. Reward successful ideas.
4. Create a comprehensive strategy for each idea that will go to market.

Level 4: Innovative Leadership:

1. Your ideas are now generating a profit.
2. Leadership in the organization are champions of the process and promote new idea generation.
3. Start projecting and forecasting your ideas to help hold your organization accountable for the future revenue.
4. Review innovations at the executive level quarterly.
5. Protect your intellectual property.

Level 5: Innovative Organization:

1. Write thought leadership articles for public consumption.
2. Speak about innovation at industry engagements.

Chapter 10

Brand Identity

"For better or for worse, our company is a reflection of my thinking, my character, my values." - Rupert Murdoch, American media powerhouse

The Vision:

The products and services we provide are top-of-mind for our customers, and we ensure every touch with our employees, customers, partners, and community have positive and trusting experiences with our organization.

What the Data Says:

- 71% of people say they are more likely to purchase a brand they follow on social media.[1]
- 63% of people searching online are likely to follow a business if they have their business info on social media.[1]
- 88% of customers will stay loyal to a brand based on quality and 50% on price.[1]

The Meaning:

Have a tenacious passion for what you build. When you're all alone, sitting in a dark room wondering why your business is failing, there is only one true thing to power you forward: You believe in your purpose and make sure everyone else follows.

Brand identity is everywhere you look. From grabbing your coffee in the morning, to reading the news, to recognizing the billboards on your way to work, it's the feeling you get when you see, taste, smell, or hear something that makes you think about a specific brand.

Companies all over the world are creating a brand identity for themselves, giving people a sense of who they are and what they represent. Your brand is the meaning behind your logo, what you do, and the message you send.

Examples:

Below are a few company examples of setbacks, success stories, and turnarounds where Brand Identity was mature or missing.

Company: Coca-Cola

The Setback: Coca-Cola underestimated the power of its brand and decided to launch a campaign to keep up with Pepsi by releasing New Coke in 1985. The decision was to terminate their most popular soft drink and replace it with a new brand in hopes of presenting Coke as fresh and better than ever. Unfortunately, customers didn't want a new brand of Coke. The company quickly reversed their decision and brought back the original Coke, but the damage to their brand was done.

Company: Cosmopolitan

The Setback: Cosmopolitan, the famous women's magazine once tried to sell products. In 1999, the launch of yogurts and cheeses had been assumed to be a huge success due to the brand's well-known name. The expensive yogurt was considered sophisticated and would justify the high price. The company assumed the brand name would be enough to sell their products successfully without doing any marketing or advertising to consumers. After 18 months, the company pulled their products and decided to stick with what they were good at: fashion publishing.

Brand Identity: What's the Diagnosis?

Symptoms:

There are several obvious signs that you may not have an effective brand. Have you considered rebranding already? Maybe you hesitate to give out your card. You should be proud of every aspect of your business. Your brand should be simple yet stand out from everyone else. It should bring to mind the deep personality of who you are and attract the customers and talent you need to be successful. If the above doesn't sound like who your company is, then perform this quick and simple assessment below.

At the writing of this book, my new company is only a couple months old. I have no brand yet but have begun to focus on a clear and crisp message. My marketing materials, social, and web presence are all consistent. I have just started helping potential customers understand who I am by networking, teaching, speaking, and writing this book. Only time will tell if I can create a brand that resonates.

The Assessment:

1. Did you get help from an experienced professional? Is your brand clear and crisp?
2. Do you have a brand built around your business and not yourself? If your brand is around yourself, is that intentional?
3. Do you have an online presence?
4. Is your brand consistent across all exposures (website, social media profiles, business cards, other marketing materials)?
5. Does your brand differentiate you from the competition? Does it convey something about your values to build an emotional connection with customers?
6. Are you consistently helping customers remember who you are? The more your prospects see you, the more likely they will contact you.
7. Does your brand attract the customers and talent you need to be successful?
8. Do you under-promise and over-deliver?

9. Does your CEO/leadership take ownership of the brand and manage it to the highest standards?
10. Can the entire organization consistently and accurately articulate the brand's promise?
11. Do customers recommend you?

Baseline Your Maturity Level:

Level 1: No identity; identity conflict:

You can't answer "Yes" to any of the questions.

Level 2: Self-awareness; not public aware:

You can answer "Yes" to the first two questions.

Level 3: Social and public awareness:

You can answer "Yes" to questions 1-5.

Level 4: You Posses Personality:

You can answer "Yes" to 1-8.

Level 5: Entrenched Customer Meaning:

You can answer "Yes" to all the questions.

Your baseline maturity level for Brand Identity is: _____

Brand Identity: Mind the Gap

Developing a strong brand identity is extremely important to your overall success. Effective branding can help you build your reputation, make you stand out from the competition, and attract the ideal clients. To portray this type of image, you must do the following:

Level 1: No identity; identity conflict:

1. Create your vision.
2. Determine your values as an organization.

Level 2: Self-awareness; not public aware:

1. Create a visual identity with all media that aligns with your vision and represents the company your target audience wants to work with.
2. Implement an effective brand management plan.

Level 3: Social and public awareness:

1. Launch your brand on all media, consistently.
2. Monitor your online reputation.
3. Ask for references.
4. Continuously network.
5. Build relationships.
6. Ensure your organization's leadership takes ownership of the brand.
7. Assign ownership to a senior leader to manage the brand.

Level 4: You Posses Personality:

1. Deliver consistently and pay attention to the details.
2. Stay present, so prospects see you, constantly.

3. Consistently evaluate your brand management plan and process.
4. Ensure all employees can consistently and accurately articulate your brand's promise.

Level 5: Entrenched Customer Meaning:

1. Stay true to yourself and maintain your values.
2. Be consistent.

Chapter 11

Collaboration

"It is literally true that you can succeed best and quickest by helping others to succeed." - Napolean Hill, American author

The Vision:

We are inclusive in thought, good at working across internal and external boundaries and leveraging our strengths to drive the best outcomes through our people, process, and technology.

What the Data Says:

- 86% of respondents blame lack of collaboration or ineffective communication for workplace failures; similarly, 92% of respondents also agree that a company's tendency to hit or miss a deadline will impact bottom line results.[1]
- Over 70% of individuals either agree or strongly agree that a lack of candor impacts the company's ability to perform optimally.[1]
- More than 97% of those surveyed believe the lack of alignment within a team directly impacts the outcome of any given task or project.[1]
- 90% of respondents believed that decision-makers should seek out other opinions before making a final decision; approximately 40% felt that leaders and decision makers consistently failed to do so.[1]
- Nearly 100% (99.1) prefer a workplace in which people identify and discuss issues truthfully and effectively, yet less than half said their organization's tendency is to do so.[1]
- Businesses lose an average of $11,000 per employee every year due to ineffective communications and collaboration.[2]

The Meaning:

We collaborate effectively through the sharing of knowledge, abilities, services, and technologies to achieve better outcomes. Collaboration best occurs by letting go of hierarchical boundaries and understanding personal and cultural differences, then by leveraging our strengths and sharing ideas across internal and external boundaries to the organization, including shareholders, partners, and customers across geopolitical boundaries.

Examples:

Below are a few company examples of setbacks, success stories, and turnarounds where Collaboration was mature or missing.

Company: A Human Services Non-Profit

The Success Story: This leading human-services non-profit organization has made a big difference for thousands of children and families in need. The organization created buy-in and collaborated across all of its stakeholders, including employees, donors, families, children, and government agencies. The result was an increase in the number of families served, high school graduation rates, and involvement in workgroups and boards.

Company: Neolistics

The Turnaround: In a culture of finger pointing and lack of accountability, collaboration was lacking. After multiple small efforts, Palentine took a larger and more drastic approach to turn around their culture of non-collaboration. Utilizing positive change management techniques with a majority of the organization, the employees walked away from a multi-day event feeling empowered after collaborating with people they had never worked with before. It allowed them to generate new and innovative approaches to improving how they did business.

Collaboration: What's the Diagnosis?

Symptoms:

Lack of collaboration could be a side effect of poor communication. This chapter assumes good communication is in place, but collaboration is lacking. How do you know if better collaboration is needed in places where lack of communication is not the cause?

Lack of collaboration can be baffling. It may seem so obvious to an outsider, but those on the inside who aren't collaborating can remain completely unaware. It's fascinating to sit back and watch the dysfunction for a while before reality kicks in, and you do something about it.

Collaboration was difficult to find at Neolistics. I remember sitting in a meeting with five of my peers from various departments. We worked well together and were creating a presentation for the leadership that would explain how we came to a conclusion and how we were going to solve a major problem. Once the presentation was where we wanted it to be, we met with another department to get their point of view. The leader of this group said, "Thank you for all your hard work. We will take it from here." The presentation and the story behind the problem were then pitched in the trash and this leader, who had not been involved with the problem, developed their own presentation and story. No matter how successful or unsuccessful the new presentation went, what mattered was the original work we did was completely disregarded. We all felt pushed aside and unworthy. How was that going to impact our ability to collaborate in the future?

How well does your company collaborate? There are entire companies that focus only on collaboration. This list below is not meant to be an exhaustive set of questions, only a gauge as to whether or not you have a problem.

There are a few questions to ask yourself to identify if this capability is lacking.

The Assessment:

People:

1. Do managers and teams share the work and the success?
2. Do you have leaders trying to promote better collaboration by bringing people together?
3. Does your organizational structure promote collaboration?
4. Are your people empowered with the knowledge and decision rights to move quickly?
5. Is your morale good?

Process:

6. Do you have processes in place where new ideas can be heard and built upon?
7. Do you understand the processes in your organization and how effective or ineffective they are to get work done?
8. Do you measure collaboration effectiveness?

Technology:

1. Do you actively use other forms of technology for collaborating other than outlook as your method of solving a problem or even performing project management?
2. Does your team have access to information to make decisions and get work done quickly?

Baseline Your Maturity Level:

Level 1: Collabor"what" Reactive Management:

You can't answer "Yes" to any of the above questions.

Level 2: Inconsistent Management:

You feel bad about answering "No" to all the questions and found one or two groups where you can say "Yes" to three or more of the above questions.

Level 3: Defined:

You answered "Yes" to 1, 2, 4, 7, and 9.

Level 4: Capability Quantitatively Managed:

You answered "Yes" to 1, 2, 4, 5, 6, 7, 9, and 10.

Level 5: Optimizing Change Management:

You answered "Yes" to all of the above.

Your baseline maturity level for Collaboration is: _____

Collaboration: Mind the Gap

After diagnosing where you are with your collaboration levels, the next steps are as follows:

Level 1: Collabor"what" Reactive Management:

At this level, you must start with the people. It doesn't matter how good your processes are or how much you spent on the coolest collaboration software if the people using it aren't ready.

1. Identify why morale is low and fix the causes.
2. Identify a core set of leaders who are naturally collaborative and set up a Tiger team (three to seven people) with these individuals to tackle collaboration. Arm them with the employee morale causes.
3. Identify areas where knowledge sharing is low and find ways to improve this. It may mean documenting processes in a place where you can share it, but ask your organization where to start first. They will appreciate it.
4. Identify where you have micro-managers and re-educate them on better leadership techniques.
5. Double check that Communication is operating at a Level 3.

Level 2: Inconsistent Management:

1. After building the first Tiger team, have them share their success with the entire organization and ask for volunteers for the next two Tiger teams. Have these next two teams tackle better understanding the processes that are slow or where silos inhibit the process. You will be amazed at how many people volunteer to be on these teams. Reward them.
2. After a few successes, have the Tiger teams share this information with the entire organization. Return to Level 2, Step 1, and begin again with two more teams.

Level 3: Defined:

1. Document your process information and share it.
2. Determine how new ideas for services, new products, and process improvements can be shared.
3. Evaluate re-organizing your space to be more collaborative. Fewer offices and shorter meetings.
4. Define how you are going to measure collaboration, then baseline it and establish a target for improvement.

Level 4: Capability Quantitatively Managed:

1. Evaluate your organizational structure and areas where collaboration is hindered due to the structure, even with collaborative managers.
2. Share your collaboration metrics, targets, and successes.

Level 5: Optimizing Change Management:

1. Ensure your technology speeds up collaboration and information sharing. Make purchases only after you have made improvements on the people side.
2. Review your collaboration metrics and actuals. Evaluate where you can make improvements and implement them.

Chapter 12

Customer Intimacy

"Exceed your customer's expectations. If you do, they'll come back, over and over. Give them what they want – and a little more. Let them know you appreciate them." - Sam Walton, American entrepreneur and founder of Walmart and Sam's Club

The Vision:

We are good at building mutually-beneficial relationships that instill enduring trust and loyalty with our customers.

What the Data Says:

- Fully engaged customers deliver a 23% premium in terms of share of wallet, profitability, revenue, and relationship growth.[1]
- 85% of companies have customer experience levels that have not reached a good level of engagement yet.[4]
- 22% plus increase was experienced in productivity when you actively engage how employees work contributes to an effective customer intimacy strategy, which has a direct effect on customer satisfaction.[5]
- 68% of customers will leave your company if they believe you don't care about them.[6]

The Meaning:

The ability to connect and build collaborative partnerships with customers must be a strength for any company to be successful. When your employees have positive and meaningful interactions with customers, intimacy is enriched and develops a long-term value for the organization that no other competitor can copy. You build customer intimacy through deep relationships, knowledge, and insight of your customer, customer service, knowledge of the customers' needs better than they understand themselves, access through multiple communication channels, and partnering to innovate and drive your customers' success. When your brand identity has formed, and it feels like a "religion," you've got it!

As mentioned earlier, customer service is a foundational capability that must exist before customer intimacy can be achieved. It assumes product and service quality, balanced with productivity, are already established. The competition can catch up when you only have maturity in quality and productivity. These capabilities are foundational and the bare minimum required for keeping your customers. Customer intimacy is required to keep your customers' loyalty for the long term.

Customers will stick with businesses that care about them, despite market conditions.

Examples:

Below are a few company examples of setbacks, success stories, and turnarounds where Customer Intimacy was mature or missing.

Company: Mercedes

The Setback and Turnaround: Mercedes used innovation, trend-setting, and enduring style to lure the digitally savvy and young, wealthy car buyers (16-33 years old) and established a strong presence on industry-leading social networks, such as Facebook and YouTube. After a slump in the eye of the recession, taking $3.5 billion in losses, Mercedes sales rose 24% worldwide the following year.[2]

Company: Tesco[3]

The Turnaround: Linking supply chain collaboration between operations and customer service with customer insights, Tesco worked out the operational details of how to deliver exactly what customers wanted to each type of store. Their agile supply chain allowed them to replenish small stores at the same cost as big stores so they could charge the same prices in every format. They continued to use insights from their Clubcard to regularly adjust offers and tweaking the supply chain accordingly. Interestingly, as soon as they rolled out home shopping, store managers saw increased sales.

Few organizations have Tesco's foundational discipline of continuous improvement, which allows them to take full advantage of the insights they can glean from analyzing customer data. Even fewer companies have the cross-functional collaboration that enables them to turn those insights into new customer experiences delivered by their supply chain. But marrying these two capabilities along with the agility to improve continuously is a competitive necessity to deliver higher levels of value to customers than was previously possible.

Company: A Japanese Pharmaceutical Company

The Success Story: This pharmaceutical company leveraged a strategic approach to align the organization behind a customer intimacy strategy. In three years, net sales increased 56%. They also became the fastest growing pharmaceutical company in Japan for three years in a row.

Customer Intimacy: What's the Diagnosis?

Symptoms:

How well do you know your prospects and your customers? How well do they know you or even your competition? How do they feel about your products and your brand? Truly knowing your customers is not just about who they are and where they work. Intimacy is being in a position to anticipate the needs of your customers before they do, ready to deliver product and service excellence every time, which wins the hearts and minds of those you serve.

The most memorable lack of customer intimacy in my experience has been when salespeople call me by the wrong name or send me an email addressed to someone else. These situations have happened numerous times. Just that small and simple lack of their attention to detail is enough to give me a poor impression of the company in everything they may do.

Some of my best customer intimacy examples come from salespeople who truly act as if they don't want anything from me. They genuinely want to get to know me, my business, what our problems are. They also know if I need them, I will ask; they don't have to push it on me. Building that type of relationship from the start is rewarded with long-time customers.

The Assessment:

1. Have you researched your ideal customers? Do you know their dreams, desires, fears, and frustrations?
2. Do you have multiple ways to reach your customers?
3. Do you have a clear picture of your customer, how they behave, how to engage them, and how/why they interact with your brand?
4. Do all your employees think outside-in? Meaning, do they think like your customers?
5. Are customers at the center of how you make decisions to ensure your alignment with your customers' needs?

6. Do you have effective organizational capabilities in values, brand identity, customer service, effective communication, and quality?
7. Do the majority of your customers refer you to other prospects?

Baseline Your Maturity Level:

Level 1: Ready to Understand:

You cannot answer "Yes" to any of the questions above.

Level 2: Alignment:

You can answer "Yes" to questions one and two.

Level 3: Optimized:

You can answer "Yes" to questions 1-3.

Level 4: Engagement:

You can answer "Yes" to questions 1-7.

Level 5: Lifetime Advocacy:

You can answer "Yes" to all the questions.

Your baseline maturity level for Customer Intimacy is: _____

Customer Intimacy: Mind the Gap

So, if 68% of your customers are willing to leave your company if they believe you don't care about them and the cost of switching companies is nominal, then that could happen tomorrow. How would that impact your revenue and bottom line? What if the time and cost for a customer to switch to a new company are long and costly, so they begin to hold you accountable for areas you have a lack of maturity. Maybe they will be more vocal on social media or begin spending more "quality" time with you and your team. How will that impact your bottom line?

After diagnosing where you are with your customer intimacy levels, the next steps are as follows:

Level 1: Ready to Understand:

1. Profile your types of customers. Understand them by reviewing blogs, articles, books, 1:1 interviews, and conversations, customer surveys.
2. Create empathy. Understand what it's like to be in your customer's shoes.

Level 2: Alignment:

1. Begin bonding to create trust. Level 1 and Level 2 could take years to build deep bonds and trust.
2. Connect your customer intimacy and experience strategy to your vision and business strategy.
3. Make sure every touch point you share with your customer is consistent and available. Align your brand identity capability.

Level 3: Optimized:

1. Continue to invest in the time with your customers. Make sure you are not out-of-site-out-of-mind. Personalize every interaction.
2. Ensure your customer service capability is an exception.
3. Collect and analyze your customer data. Evaluate and solve problem areas.

Level 4: Engagement:

1. Leverage all social media networks to connect with your customers.
2. Create metrics and targets for customer engagement.
3. Evaluate customer trends to your advantage.
4. Survey your customer base.

Level 5: Lifetime Advocacy:

1. Know who your VIP and advocate customers are.
2. Provide incentives for customer referrals.

Chapter 13

Customer Service

> *"You'll never have a product or price advantage again. They can be easily duplicated, but a strong customer service culture can't be copied."* - Jerry Fritz, customer experience speaker and author

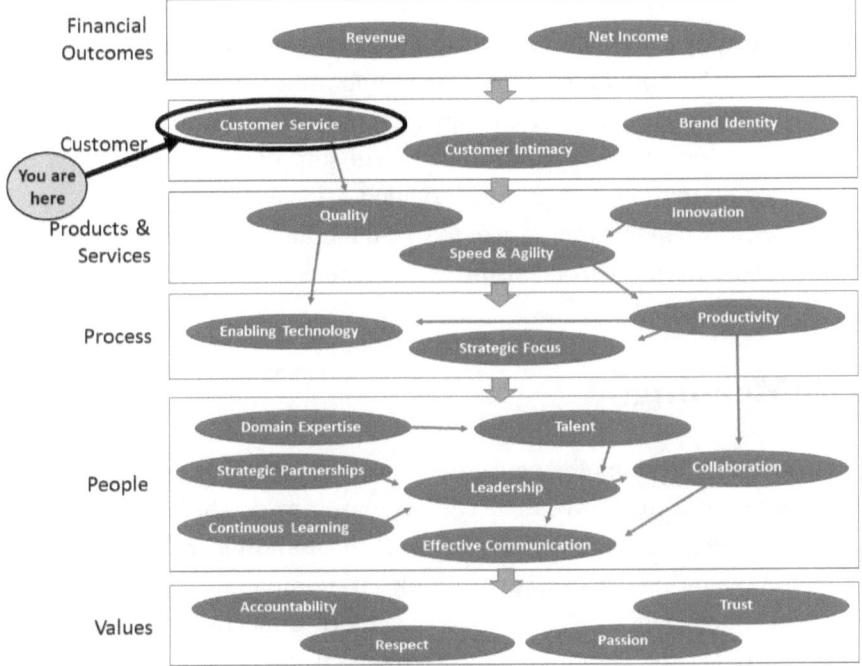

The Vision:

We provide consistent service that forms positive images in the minds of our employees and customers. This service yields high levels of brand loyalty and creates value for our customers.

What the Data Says:

- 78% of consumers have bailed on a transaction or not made an intended purchase because of a poor service experience.[2]
- On average, loyal customers are worth up to 10 times as much as their first purchase.[2]
- Probability of selling to an existing customer is 60-70%; probability of selling to a new prospect is 5-20%.[2]
- It takes 12 positive experiences to make up for one unresolved negative experience.[2]
- 59% of Americans would try a new brand or company for a better service experience.[2]
- A study from NewVoiceMedia indicates that companies lose more than $62 billion each year due to poor customer service.[3]
- 52% of disgruntled customers spout off to family and friends; an even more astounding 32% will stop doing business with the company altogether that provided a lousy customer experience. And when customers take to social media to air their experiences, more than 60% of consumers are influenced by these detrimental comments.[4]

The Meaning:

With so many options for consumers, customers will remain loyal to a company only if they have a very good reason to do so. Because of this, providing the best customer service is key to building trust and loyalty. With many studies and surveys completed, companies continue to find that consumers rate customer service as more important than price. To consistently get the right experience, many customers are willing to pay more. Lastly, word of mouth is the most powerful marketing tool you have. What other customers say can make or break your business.

Examples:

Below are a few company examples of setbacks, success stories, and turnarounds where Customer Service was mature or missing.

Company: Bethlehem Steel

The Setback: Bethlehem Steel was a major part of American history. Bethlehem Steel was the backbone of the first blasting furnace, railroads, skyscrapers, coal, nuclear reactors, warships, cargo vessels, large construction projects like arenas, and other major infrastructural accomplishments. However, the company never adjusted to the new service-based economy that gained ground in the 1990s. Cheap imports worsened the situation. Bethlehem Steel, disappeared forever when it filed for bankruptcy in 2001.[5]

Company: US Airways

The Setback: Before US Airways was purchased by America West in 2005, the airline slashed its customer service budget, and outsourced many of those functions. As a result, the company mishandled or failed to address numerous complaints, angering customers to the point that no amount of cost-cutting could make up for the fact that passengers no longer wanted to do business with the airline, eventually forcing it to file bankruptcy.[1]

Company: InfoSys

The Success Story: InfoSys views its clients as key stakeholders in fulfilling its long-term goals, so the company considers it critical to be strategically aligned with each one of its clients. The company developed an approach to managing their clients that established a transparent approach to ensuring quality, customer service, and customer satisfaction. With this approach, InfoSys increased the number of active clients from 293 to 500. The number of accounts exceeding $20M annually increased almost 4x.

Customer Service: What's the Diagnosis?

Symptoms:

How does bad customer service feel? Be the customer for a bit. The worst outcome for your business is the loss of a customer. Customer satisfaction is low. Negative press or word of mouth. And now with social media touching billions of people, you simply cannot afford for those comments to go viral.

We've all had experiences of good and bad customer service as consumers. If I could just go to Starbucks all the time to get what I need, I know I am going to get the same, consistent, wonderful customer service every time, no matter which store I visit. Sometimes it's easy just to say, "I am not going back." But in other situations, the cost and ease to change to a new provider are challenging. Currently, I am thinking of the memory care facility where my mom is living. My mom and her family, from my point of view, would be the customers for the facility. While the employees are all very kind, from my vantage point, they do not provide good care for their residents. For example, my mom has a habit of playing with the creases in her pants when she sits in a chair. If she is at the table for a meal, she will play with these creases instead of eating. I have asked every staff member to please push her up to the table so she can't see her pants, just the food in front of her. It is still happening, and she continues to lose weight because she doesn't remember to eat. When she is pushed up to the table properly, she doesn't forget to eat because that's all she sees.

The Assessment:

1. Do you track the quality and speed of delivery of your products and services?
2. Do you track customer satisfaction with your products and services?
3. Do you review the feedback from your customers?
4. Do you improve metrics and feedback received from your customers?
5. Is your staff attentive to the customer?
6. Does your staff behave appropriately around the customer?

7. Have you established customer service expectations with your staff?
8. Do you have a customer service practice?
9. Have you integrated your brand identity and customer intimacy capabilities with customer service?
10. Does your staff have effective communication capabilities?
11. Do you have an established productivity capability?

Baseline Your Maturity Level:

Level 1: Reactive:

You are unable to answer "Yes" to any of the questions. You are in a reactive state where there is little or no formal process/practice in place.

Level 2: Tracking:

You can answer "Yes" to number one and two above. Your organization collects the data to track specific metrics on your customers and feedback.

Level 3: Accountable Service:

You can answer "Yes" to questions 1-4. Your organization utilized the customer data and had established targets for the metrics you collect. For customers who give negative feedback, you have a process for resolution.

Level 4: Integrated Service:

You can answer "Yes" to questions 1-9. Your organization leverages the feedback and metrics, as well as data from your customer intimacy and brand identity capabilities. You have active programs to improve your staff in immediate contact with the customer to ensure they deliver the service expected.

Level 5: Best Practice:

You can answer "Yes" to all the questions. Your customer service capability is strong and aligned with productivity, collaboration, effective communication, brand identity, and customer intimacy.

Your baseline maturity level for Customer Service is: _____

Customer Service: Mind the Gap

After diagnosing where you are with your customer service levels, the next steps are as follows:

Level 1: Reactive:

1. Identify the metrics you want to track.
2. Put the systems in place to track the metrics.
3. Identify the problem areas and prioritize for improvements.
4. Establish a customer service plan.

Level 2: Tracking:

1. Review the metrics and feedback collected.
2. Continue to identify the problem areas and prioritize for improvements.
3. Integrate customer service into your business strategy.

Level 3: Accountable Service:

1. Get all your departments involved in improving customer service.
2. Establish expectations for staff performance plans to increase accountability.
3. Provide incentives for modeling excellence in customer service.
4. Collaborate with marketing and sales to understand your customers' needs.
5. Review your customer service practices and document the processes.

Level 4: Integrated Service:

1. Review your customer service processes for effectiveness.
2. Integrate productivity and quality capabilities with customer service.

3. Integrate brand identity and customer intimacy capabilities.
4. Leverage enabling technology to be effective and efficient.

Level 5: Best Practice:

1. Integrate productivity and effective communication capabilities.
2. Continuously review your customer service practices and improve.

Chapter 14

Speed and Agility

"Success today requires the agility and drive to constantly rethink, reinvigorate, react, and reinvent." ~ Bill Gates, American businessman, author and co-founder of Microsoft

The Vision:

We act quickly when opportunities arise or risks need to be managed. Whether this is to expand into new markets, create new products and services, mitigate risks, or improve business processes, acting with speed is key.

What the Data Says:

- 70% of agile companies rank in the top 25% of organizational health.[1]
- 90% of executives ranked organizational agility both as critical to business success and as growing in importance over time.[2]

The Meaning:

Speed is paramount if your organization is going to thrive and achieve success. To be speedy, stabilizing and consistent processes are foundational to sustain the speed for any length of time. If your organization is not fast, your competitors will be. And the faster you learn, the faster you evolve. When you have speed and agility with your business practices, your innovation and productivity go through the roof. The goal is to boost the odds of beating the competition to the market and delighting your customers along the way. We do this by putting consistent quality systems in place that produce the products and services you deliver while having the information available to spot additional opportunities.

Examples:

Below are a few company examples of setbacks, success stories, and turnarounds where Speed and Agility were mature or missing.

Company: Blockbuster

The Setback: Not only did Blockbuster make a huge mistake by refusing to buy Netflix. They also strongly believed the DVD-by-mail service was never going to work, and stuck to their physical movie rental service. Blockbuster remained stagnant for years while Netflix found ways to move the entire industry forward. Blockbuster filed for bankruptcy in 2010 and the following its remaining stores were bought by Dish Network. Only a handful of a few Blockbuster franchises remain today.

Company: A US Supplier

The Success Story: A US supplier of metal buildings and roofing products, achieved great speed and efficiency with the company's business processes. Originally, each of the company's branches operated in their own way, and those differences led to costly inconsistencies. With their focus, the company achieved an increase in the percentage of orders delivered within ten days of promised date by 9% and the percentage of orders with quality problems decreased by 37%.

Speed and Agility: What's the Diagnosis?

Symptoms:

A lack of business agility is painful. Everything just feels slow. You may even feel that you don't have the ability to make decisions or there is too much bureaucracy to move products, deliver services, and change the business. You know something is wrong, but you can't quite put your finger on it.

At Neolistics, while there were other immature capabilities, speed and agility truly suffered the most. The lack of multiple root cause capabilities had a compounding effect on speed. As an example, from an outside view from the department, a customer-looking-in point of view, I go back to the time it takes to build a server example in the Productivity chapter. From the inside, the employees in the division delivering the server did not feel productive and little could be accomplished while it was taking so long to complete a task. Outside the division, from the customer's point of view, all they knew was it was taking far too long. Our customers didn't know newer technologies would significantly accelerate this process, but our employees did. The customers did, however, recall previous faster experiences. Also, because the process was going so slow, we were risking missing key deadlines. This gave the division unwanted attention which only increased frustration towards to the ineffective process.

This example at Neolistics shouldn't be foreign to you. I have witnessed similar experiences at multiple companies, and my colleagues share similar stories. I would imagine you can name a few processes at your own company where productivity or other root cause capabilities are impacting your speed and agility.

The Assessment:

Unfortunately, the root cause is typically in one of the other capabilities. For the assessment, check the symptoms and then the organizational capabilities.

1. Do you have any of these values lacking:
   Trust|Integrity|Honesty|Respect|Passion|Purpose|Accountability
2. Do you have poor morale or lots of conflicts? Do you have effective Leadership in place?
3. Do you have key positions not filled or missing skills? Do you have the Talent you need?
4. Are meetings unproductive? Are you failing to deliver the intended message? Does your business Communicate Effectively?
5. Are people not working together well? Is your organization Collaborative?
6. Are there too many conflicting priorities? Do you have Strategic Focus?
7. Do things feel a bit slow? Do you need the approval of several people to get anything done? Is your organization Productive?
8. Do you feel you could automate or improve the quality of what you're delivering? Are you leveraging Enabling Technology?
9. Do you have defects in what you are creating? Either they are already in the market, and you need to fix them, or you are finding them and need to fix them before your product goes out the door. Do you have an effective Quality capability?
10. Do you have a long list of improvements you haven't made to speed up and improve the quality of your processes and their outputs?

Baseline Your Maturity Level:

Level 1: Molasses:

If you answer "Yes" to one and two, stop here. Values and Leadership are foundational to the next steps.

Level 2: Defined:

Values and Leadership are effective, and you don't have any missing Talent. Communication is effective in the organization. You answered "No" to questions 1–4.

Level 3: Managed:

Values, Leadership, Talent, Communication, Collaboration, and Strategic Focus are well managed. You answered "No" to questions 1–6.

Level 4: Capability Quantitatively Managed:

Values, Leadership, Talent, Communication, Collaboration, Strategic Focus, Productive, and Enabling Technology are well managed. You answered "No" to questions 1–9.

Level 5: Optimizing:

Values, Leadership, Talent, Communication, Collaboration, Strategic Focus, Productive, and Enabling Technology are well managed, and Quality is under control. You are consistently improving in all of the questions.

Your baseline maturity level for Speed and Agility is: _____

Speed and Agility: Mind the Gap

While simply stated, it is not a Speedy road to recovery depending on your level of maturity and the size of your organization.

After diagnosing where you are with your speed and agility levels, the next steps are as follows:

Level 1: Molasses:

1. Review the chapters on Values and Leadership. Get to Level 3 for Values and Leadership confidently before you move forward to the next level below.

Level 2: Defined:

1. Get to Level 3 with your Talent. Make sure you have the key positions filled where Speed and Agility are critical.
2. Review the chapter on Effective Communication and achieve Level 3 confidently.

Level 3: Managed:

1. Review the chapter on Collaboration and get to Level 3.
2. Review the chapter on Strategic Focus and get to Level 3.

Level 4: Capability Quantitatively Managed:

1. Review the chapter on Productivity and get to Level 3.
2. Review the chapter on Enabling Technology and get to Level 3.

Level 5: Optimizing:

1. Review the chapter on Quality and make sure you are at Level 3.
2. Continuously improve on each of the capabilities above and strive for level 4, then 5. Don't let any of them slide back to Level 1 or 2 or you will infect the rest of the capabilities and must start over.

Chapter 15

Quality

"Quality is everyone's responsibility." - W. Edwards Deming, American engineer, author, and professor

The Vision:

We provide a consistent level of quality in our products and services that fully satisfy the requirements in the minds of our employees and customers. It builds and yields high levels of brand loyalty and long-term value for the organization and our customers.

What the Data Says:

- Research shows that the costs of poor quality can range from 15%-40% of business costs (e.g., rework, returns or complaints, reduced service levels, lost revenue).[1]
- The average organization surveyed by Gartner said it loses $8.2 million annually through poor data quality. Furthermore, of the 140 companies surveyed, 22% estimated their annual losses resulting from bad data at $20 million. 4% put that figure as high as an astounding $100 million.[3]

The Meaning:

Customers expect you to deliver quality products. If you do not, they will quickly look for alternatives. Quality is critical to satisfying your customers and retaining their loyalty, so they continue to buy from you in the future. Quality products make an important contribution to long-term revenue and profitability. They also enable you to charge and maintain higher prices.

The cost of poor quality is just too high. Without an effective quality control system in place, you may incur the cost of analyzing non-conforming goods or services to determine the root causes and retesting products and services after reworking them. In some cases, you may have to scrap defective products or work and incur additional costs to replace them. If defective products reach customers, you will have to pay for returns and replacements and, in serious cases, you could incur legal costs for failure to comply with customer or industry standards. Indeed, the cost of poor quality increases the further you move down the value stream of your company to produce your goods and services.

Examples:

Below are a few company examples of setbacks, success stories, and turnarounds where Quality was mature or missing.

Company: Wendy's

The Setback and Turnaround: Dave Thomas retired as Wendy's CEO in 1982, 13 years after founding what had become one of the largest fast-food chains in the U.S. Within years, the company revenues dropped as some customers were unimpressed with a new breakfast menu, and cleanliness and service standards slipped within franchises. James Near became the company's top executive upon Thomas' retirement to manage the company's turnaround. Thomas also came out of retirement to be the company's spokesman in its advertisements, leading one of the company's most successful advertising campaigns.

Company: Ford

The Setback: In response to competition from Japanese imports, Ford released the Pinto in 1971, a popular automotive icon that looked to capture consumer hearts with its $2,000 price-tag.

The Pinto's aesthetic quality was in question. In 1977, however, lawsuits emerged involving allegations of a structural design fault. The fuel tank was near the rear bumper and rear axle, meaning that rear-end collisions would elevate the risk of fires.

Ford's decision to recall 1.4 million units in 1978 saved no face as an investigative journalist, Mark Dowie, revealed that Ford had been aware of the design flaw during production. He published a cost-benefit analysis document that Ford compared the cost of $11 per-vehicle repairs with the cost of settlements for deaths, injuries, and burnouts. The loss of life and loss in sales cost the company over $137.5M.[2]

Company: Johnson & Johnson

The Setback: Johnson & Johnson recalled 300 million items including bottles of Children's Tylenol, Benadryl, Motrin, and a dozen other products in April 2010. The source of trouble with Tylenol and Motrin was due to quality control at the facilities operated by company division, McNeil Consumer Healthcare. Some industry estimates place the sales of the children's version of Tylenol down by as much as 90% because of the news about the dangers of the product.

Quality: What's the Diagnosis?

Symptoms:

Poor quality is not always an attribute of the software or a product. It could be in the proposals you provide or invoices you send. If you continue to make mistakes, your customers will eventually leave. For example, I used to hold many events at a local events facility with a few of the professional organizations where I am a member. The exposure the facility received from these events could potentially bring in more business. However, I eventually stopped doing business with them because it would take me months of in-person conversations, emails, and phone calls to resolve errors in our billing. There were multiple errors in how our events were set up even though it was documented in our contract and there was poor follow up from the manager. When I look back on the year, I think to myself "what capabilities were missing?" Keep in mind, this situation is all from my point of view, the customer, of course. I don't have insight into every angle. So, let's analyze the situation based on a few organizational capabilities:

Leadership: Started out good until the first leader of the events department left. Things then went downhill over the year.

Effective Communication: The right hand didn't know what the left hand was doing. Finger-pointing back and forth would occur between events, catering, and billing. When the leadership changed, how our events were set up changed. Even with the detailed documentation and agreements already in place, these were not followed.

Quality: The charges on the invoices were not accurate 50% of the time. Even after I would review and provide feedback ahead of time. I am still not certain if we over- or underpaid.

Customer Satisfaction: Started high at the beginning of the year, then ended low.

Overall, the loss of on-going revenue for them because we moved our events: $18,000.

While this alone seems like a small amount for many organizations, this may also be happening to other customers. The total lost opportunity cost could be much larger.

The Assessment:

1. Is your customer satisfaction high?
2. Do you have a low return rate or defect rate on your product and services?
3. Do you measure your quality, both customer satisfaction, and defects, with your core value stream?
4. Do you have the Domain Expertise for your products and services?
5. Have you automated your process to reduce manual effort?
6. Do you review your processes for effectiveness?
7. Are schedules for delivery realistic?
8. Do you have ISO certifications where you need them?

Baseline Your Maturity Level:

Level 1: Initial:

You answered "No" to all questions above. Your processes are unpredictable, poorly controlled, and reactive.

Level 2: Managed:

You answered "Yes" to questions 1-4. Processes are defined for your value stream, but there's still too much reactivity.

Level 3: Defined:

You confidently answered "Yes" to questions 1-5. Processes are documented, and people are trained to perform them. You know your customer satisfaction rate and defect rates.

Level 4: Capability Quantitatively Managed:

You answered "Yes" somewhat confidently to questions 1-7. Processes are measured and controlled.

Level 5: Optimizing:

You answered "Yes" to all the questions. There is a focus on continuous process improvement.

Your baseline maturity level for Quality is: _____

Quality: Mind the Gap

After diagnosing where you are with your quality levels, the next steps are as follows:

Level 1: Initial:

Processes are unpredictable, poorly controlled, and reactive. Stop the bleeding. This level is the most comprehensive; please avoid shortcuts.

1. Prioritize the critical functions/key processes.
2. Document each key process in your value stream and test to ensure your documentation is accurate.

Level 2: Managed:

Processes are defined for your value stream, but there's still too much reactivity.

1. Identify metrics for each key process for your value stream, both leading and lagging, how you will calculate each measure, and where the data will come from for the following areas:
   a. Quality
   b. Customer satisfaction

Level 3: Defined:

Processes are documented, and people are trained to perform them. You know your customer satisfaction rate and defect rates.

1. Document each key sub-process in your value stream and test to ensure your documentation is accurate.
2. Train all staff on the processes.

Level 4: Capability Quantitatively Managed:

Processes are measured and controlled.

1. Create a dashboard with your key metrics from Level 3 above. Review the metrics with team members using the processes and with leadership.

Level 5: Optimizing:

There is a focus on continuous process improvement.

1. Discuss opportunities for improvement with team members by evaluating root causes for defects and strategies for improved success.
2. Prioritize the opportunities.
3. Continuously improve all processes, competencies, knowledge, etc. from earlier levels.

Chapter 16

Enabling Technology

"The first rule of any technology used in a business is that automation applied to an efficient operation will magnify the efficiency. The second is that automation applied to an inefficient operation will magnify the inefficiency." - *Bill Gates*

The Vision:

We leverage the right technology at the right time to effectively deliver on our vision.

What the Data Says:

- 90% of security incidents are due to software defects, and your employees are opening the doors.[1]
- 63% of restaurant owners and managers said they'd invest in technology if it made their day-to-day operations more efficient.[2]
- If all entities that did business with the University of Houston System were paid via ACH, the university could save $100,000 per year.[3]
- Cloud usage continues to rise annually according to the Society of Information Management.[4]

The Meaning:

For some companies that don't sell technology products and services, enabling technology could be key to strategic success. The technology can also come in the form of equipment, and methodologies that when leveraged together, have the potential to drive radical change in the performance of employees and improve culture. A company's greatest strength that boosts performance can also be its most critical weakness if left unattended.

Examples:

Below are a few company examples of setbacks, success stories, and turnarounds where Enabling Technology was mature or missing.

Company: Target and Home Depot

The Setback: Greater than $500M loss after data breaches.

Company: Equifax

The Setback: A failure to patch a two-month-old bug led to the breach that exposed sensitive data for as many as 143 million U.S. consumers. This situation occurred via the exploitation of a web application vulnerability leveraging Apache Struts, a framework (enabling technology) used by developers creating Java-based applications. This was a risk that many companies have overlooked and had not mitigated up till this event occurred with Equifax.

Enabling Technology: What's the Diagnosis?

Symptoms:

"There has got to be an easier way," is what I would say to myself. Technology capability is growing exponentially, and if you think there's an easier way, there are probably at least ten.

When I first started at Baltic, we were managing major projects with email. It would take me forever to review an email stream and see what had been done., what problems existed, and determining who was doing what. Finding the right email was even more difficult. when hundreds existed. Then we installed two productivity tools to manage our work and share information. To this day, it's still an amazing feeling the relief this gave our team so many years ago.

All of our projects, including the tasks, progress, and associated documentation, existed within these two tools. We were able to speed up communication and productivity by having everything in one spot. It was amazing. When the rest of the company started seeing our productivity from using these tools, they wanted to jump on board as well and use them for their normal business processes. *Absolutely!* What was once deployed as a technology tool for a couple of hundred people was now an enterprise tool being used by thousands globally.

The Assessment:

1. Are vulnerabilities taken care of in the technology you use for your business, reducing your exposure to hackers?
2. Have you automated as much of your manual effort as possible?
3. Are errors reduced because of your technology?
4. Have you integrated your systems to reduce re-entry of information?
5. Do you leverage your data to benefit your business?
6. Do you have the right Talent to take care of your technology?
7. Is all the technology you use for your business cost-effective?
8. Does your technology prepare you for the future?

9. Do you leverage your technology to make business decisions?
10. Are you staff trained to use your business technology effectively?

Baseline Your Maturity Level:

Level 1: Not Enabled:

You can't answer "Yes" to any of the questions above.

Level 3: Somewhat Enabled:

You can answer "Yes" to 50% of the questions above.

Level 5: Highly Enabled and Effective:

You can answer "Yes" to 80% of the questions.

Your baseline maturity level for Enabling Technology is: _____

Enabling Technology: Mind the Gap

After diagnosing where you are with your enabling technology levels, the next steps are as follows:

Level 1: Not Enabled:

1. Identify the most critical business technology you have today. This could be, for example, your financial and time tracking systems.
2. Determine if your most critical business technology is patched and kept up-to-date to reduce security vulnerabilities.
3. Determine if your staff is trained on the effective use of your technology.
4. Ensure your technology staff is at the appropriate level to handle your technology needs.

Level 3: Somewhat Enabled:

1. Do you have overlapping uses of technology? If so, determine if you can reduce the number of technology you have serving similar business needs.
2. Train staff on the effective use of the technology you have.
3. Explore more cost-effective technology options to replace what you have.
4. Determine if cloud technology would be beneficial.
5. Ensure your business processes are best supported by the technology you utilize.

Level 5: Highly Enabled and Effective:

1. Identify the business technology you have and need for making business decisions, then create transparent self-service reporting for those who need the information.
2. Integrate systems to remove any manual re-entry of information.

Chapter 17

Strategic Partnerships

"I love creating partnerships; I love not having to bear the entire burden of the creative storytelling, and when I have unions like with George Lucas and Peter Jackson, it's really great; not only do I benefit, but the project is better for it." - Steven Spielberg, American director, producer, and screenwriter

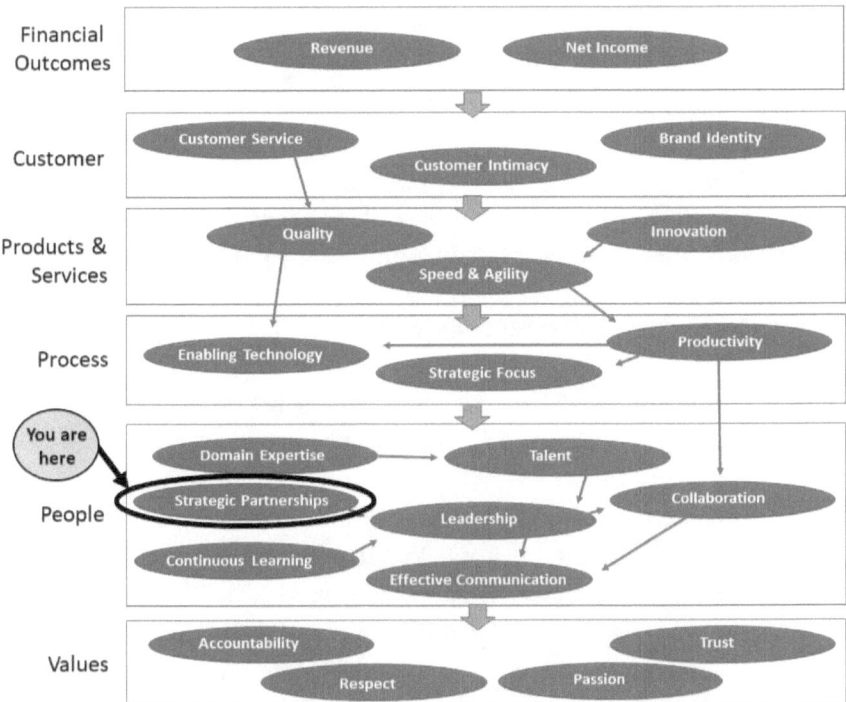

The Vision:

We leverage mutually beneficial partnerships to effectively deliver our vision.

What the Data Says:

- 80% of all business partnerships fail. That includes partnerships between individuals and entire companies.[1]

The Meaning:

As a business, we can't do everything ourselves. We must focus on our core business strengths and leverage our partners to fill in the gaps in our abilities to deliver effectively, create synergies, and give our business a competitive advantage that increases potential. Partnering successfully gives our business access to additional resources and competencies we don't have, growth in the customer base, to gain access to new products and services, and the ability to reach new markets.

Examples:

Below are a few company examples of setbacks, success stories, and turnarounds where Strategic Partnerships were mature or missing.

Company: Martha Stewart

The Setback and Turnaround: After being convicted for lying about the reason for selling her biotechnology stock two years earlier, Martha Stewart was sent to prison. Immediately after the court date, her company stock fell 22%. After being released, Martha formed partnerships with such companies as Lowes and Kodak. In 2006, her company reported $61.1 million in revenues, grew 48% from the same time the prior year. She continued to create partnerships, including JCPenney, Walmart, Michaels, Target, and Macy's, just to name a few.

Company: Borders

The Setback: The release of the Amazon Kindle in 2007 and the lag in Borders releasing their e-reader in 2010 definitely hurt the company. But many say it was a 2001 deal with Amazon that was the final down fall of Borders. A decision to pay Amazon.com to run the Borders website essentially established a way for Amazon to gain new customers, thereby funneling business away from Borders. I would suggest this was definitely not a mutually beneficial partnership.

Strategic Partnerships: What's the Diagnosis?

Symptoms:

The focus of this chapter is based on a balanced partnership. It either is or isn't.

During a conversation with a colleague, they had three key partners that provided managed services for their company. Their ability to change any of these partners were difficult, and their service was sub-optimal at best. They knew it would be difficult to change providers, so speed, quality, and cost were consistent issues. If you had any project involving one of these providers, it was well known to double your time estimates just because follow up, meetings, and the work would take longer than planned. Does this sound like any of your strategic partners?

The Assessment:

1. Do you and your partner(s) have fair and balanced roles and responsibilities?
2. Do you agree on the finances?
3. Are all issues settled between you and your partner(s)?
4. Do you have to wait long to get a response to communications (emails, phone calls, etc.)?
5. Do you have overall effective communication with your partner(s)?
6. Do each of your partner(s) take responsibility when they should?
7. Do you have a partnership agreement with alignment in your operating terms?
8. Do your businesses complement each other?
9. Does your partnership business have a common shared vision and goals?
10. Do you align with the values of your partnership and business?
11. Do you get consistent information no matter who you talk to at the partnering business?

Baseline Your Maturity Level:

Level 1: Unbalanced Partnership:

You can't answer "Yes" to the questions above.

Level 5: Fair, Balanced, and Profitable Partnership:

Your answers to all of the questions above really should be "Yes."

Your baseline maturity level for Strategic Partnerships is: _____

Strategic Partnerships: Mind the Gap

After diagnosing where you are with your strategic partnership levels, the next steps are as follows:

Level 1: Unbalanced Partnership:

1. Revisit the role and responsibilities. Ensure authority, responsibility, time involved, and ownership of outcomes are aligned with your expectations as a partnership.
2. Ensure the decision-making on how you spend money and the revenue you target are aligned.
3. Resolve any outstanding issues and how those disagreements should be settled.
4. Create or revisit your partnership agreement. Include time off, expenses, the type of work you will take on, contingency, and exit strategy.
5. Create a partnership scorecard, one that measures the successes of the partnership that are mutually beneficial.
6. Continuously focus on building a relationship with your partners based on trust, transparency, effective communication, collaboration, and accountability.

Level 5: Fair, Balanced, and Profitable Partnership:

1. Revisit your partnership agreement yearly.
2. Evaluate the measures of success with your partner quarterly.

Chapter 18

Effective Communication

"Trust is the glue of life. It's the most essential ingredient in effective communication. It's the foundational principle that holds all relationships." - Stephen Covey, American educator and author

"Wise men speak because they have something to say; Fools because they have to say something." – Plato, classical Greek philosopher

The Vision:

We are multi-faceted and effectively communicate in a manner that is clear, consistent, inclusive and respectful that ultimately demonstrates "one voice."

What the Data Says:

- Only 1/3 of emails are opened.[1]
- 95% of texts are read within three minutes of being sent, and texts have a 99+% open rate.[1]
- Communication is 93% non-verbal (7% spoken words; 38% tone, 55% non-verbal cue).
- 31% of employees never use the company intranet.[2]
- 60% of communications teams don't measure their internal communications.[2]
- Businesses that communicate effectively are 50% more likely to have low employee turnover rates.[3]
- Nearly 15% of employees' total work time is wasted on inefficient communications. Businesses with 500 employees could be losing $5M annually.[4]

The Meaning:

The organization has the confidence that every message and experience that customers and employees have with your organization rings true and leaves the right impression or achieves the intended outcome. You utilize the right tools and resources needed for the organization to create and sustain an environment that engages and creates high productivity.

Examples:

Below are a few company examples of setbacks, success stories, and turnarounds where Effective Communication was mature or missing.

Company: Toyota

The Setback: By the time Toyota finally decided to recall millions of cars due to faulty brakes, it was already too late. After downplaying the problem for as long as possible, their hand was forced when Consumer Reports withdrew their recommendations of eight Toyota vehicles. Although the situation was eventually fully handled, failing to accept responsibility from the outset affected how customers perceived Toyota's brand.[6]

Company: British Petroleum

The Setback: The blowout of the Deepwater Horizon offshore oil rig, in April 2010, resulted in a massive crisis for BP and its partners. Among the key factors that contributed to the disaster were "poor communications" and a failure "to share important information," according to a report on the White House commission that studied the incident.[5]

Effective Communication: What's the Diagnosis?

Symptoms:

Poor communicators often feel frustrated that they don't get feedback when they present their ideas, explain something, wait for comments or questions, and still get nothing. Unfortunately, most poor communicators have little self-awareness on this topic and feel everyone else is the problem.

Now, what if this is the problem with the entire company? Imagine the impact that has on the growth of new ideas and execution of your strategy. Ineffective communication causes and worsens relationships, putting employees in a state of "fight" (argue with the one communicating) or "flight" (removing themselves from the situation either physically, emotionally, or both). These eventually become barriers to resolving problems and moving forward. Look closely at the root causes of communication problems. More often you will find that what looks like poor communication is only a symptom of a more foundational problem (look at the organizational capability map to see if there are other root capabilities), such as poor leadership, and lack of values in respect or trust.

Have you ever had someone tell you that you are not communicating well? What they could be saying is they don't "trust" you to listen or to provide information.

Have you ever sat across from your boss in your one-on-one while they text on their phone continuously? How about in a staff meeting? What kind of message does that communicate? What if your boss passes you in the hallway and doesn't look at you or say hello even when no one else is around on a regular basis? Do you have employees that send a "flaming" email? How about that email you wrote too quickly and the wording was not quite right.

A colleague of mine, Greg, experienced unfortunate circumstances when the wording in his email was taken incorrectly and it looked like he was covering up a problem. When an additional email was sent out by an employee reinforcing the wrong intent, Greg didn't correct it, and the outcome was definitely not what he intended.

The Assessment:

1. Is everyone engaged in meetings? Meaning, everyone is sharing, electronics are not in use? Look at a cross-section of meetings involving your leaders first.
2. Does the left hand know what the right hand is doing?
3. When your leadership communicates, is the information received what they intended?
4. Are people receptive to communicating problems and having open conversations?
5. Do your employees know, as a collective, the organizational mission, vision, and values from memory?
6. Do you score well on employee surveys as it pertains to effective communication?
7. Is your leadership effective at active listening?
8. Do you have a solid foundation of other root organizational capabilities, such as Leadership and Values?
9. Do you leverage effective tools to facilitate communication that start with the most personally interactive first: in person, video, phone, IM, email or letter.

Baseline Your Maturity Level:

Level 1: Look Deeper:

You can't answer "Yes" to any of the questions. It is not episodic and more systemic.

Level 3: Optimizing:

For your leadership, you can answer "Yes" to questions 1-4.

Level 5: Effective:

You can answer "Yes" to all the questions for 90% of your leadership.

Once you have assessed where you are with your leadership team, go back and evaluate the rest of your organization. I would anticipate the score will be lower than the leadership score.

Your baseline maturity level for Communication is: _____

Effective Communication: Mind the Gap

At any level of maturity for Effective Communication, closing the gap and continuous evaluation become foundational for success. I recommend you perform all these steps continuously.

1. Assess your highest leadership levels in the organization. Give this to the leaders and their direct reports and peers who are in active contact with the leader. Consolidate the results and create a development plan that may include basic skills in listening, speaking, questioning, being aware of body language, facial expressions, mood, and natural behavioral tendencies and sharing feedback.
2. Based on the assessment, determine if there are other root causes of any ineffective communication, such as lack of self-awareness or emotional intelligence. If there are other root causes, these must be dealt with first, or any educational improvements on communication will be lost if the person does not believe they have a problem to begin with. Knowing how to read between the lines in conversations can help you spot problems at work and home before they arise. Show empathy. It is a powerful display of listening.
3. In parallel organizationally, if your employees do not know the Mission, Vision, and Values by heart, create a foundation for Effective Communications with your Mission, Vision, and Values. Leaders display the importance of communications by clearly communicating a mission that is inspiring and instills a sense of purpose, a vision that conveys the goals for the organization, and the values by which your organization will operate. The obvious benefits are that you will communicate more effectively, saving both time and money.
4. Create an Organizational Communications Plan: Leaders need to convey the right information at the right time to the right people using the right communication channels. Employees need to hear a consistent message, one that helps them understand what's in it for them. Changing your words too much will make them feel as

if you are changing direction. Validate your intent and what you communicated was well understood. Know your audience. What do they want or need to hear, not what you want to tell them? Know their knowledge level. Understand what they will expect from the communication and anticipate their questions. Leverage the Minto Pyramid Principle when necessary.

5. Periodically, survey your organization's employees on communication. Review the results and make improvements.

Chapter 19
Values

"I have no special talent. I am only passionately curious."
- Albert Einstein, theoretical physicist

"It is not only what we do, but also what we do not do, for which we are accountable." – Molière, French playwright

"You can't force someone to respect you, but you can refuse to be disrespected." - Anonymous

"Trust is the foundation of Leadership" - John Maxwell

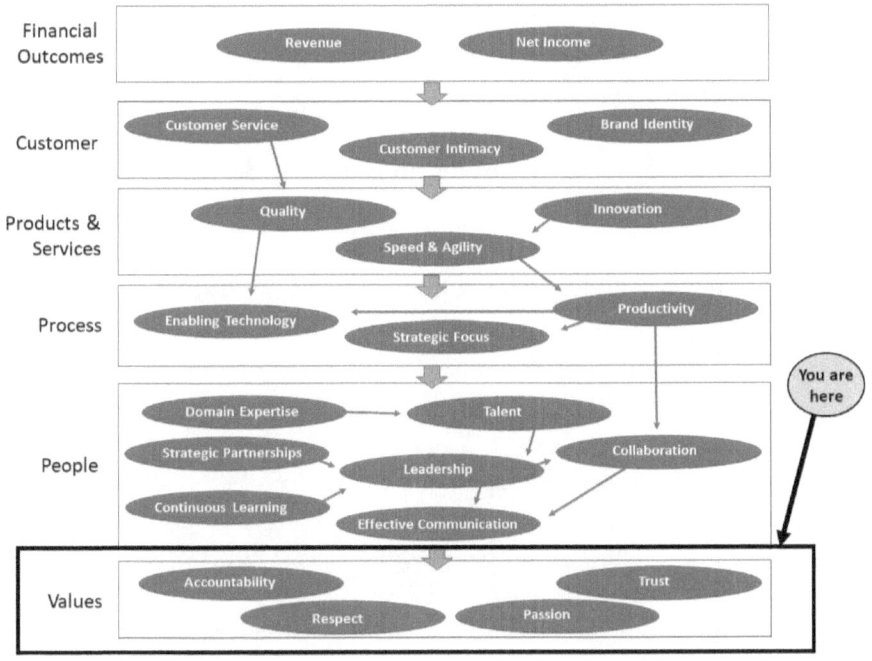

The Vision:

We are committed to being accountable to ourselves, each other, our organization, and our community behaving with integrity and showing respect to everyone, every day.

What the Data Says:

Trust|Integrity|Honesty:

- High trust companies report 74% less stress than people in low-trust companies, 106% more energy at work, 50% higher productivity, 29% more satisfied with their lives, and 40% less burnout in their jobs. People in high-trust companies reported feeling 76% more engaged.[1]

Respect|Passion|Purpose:

- Engagement in work, which is associated with feeling valued, secure, supported, and respected. Disengagement is costly. Disengaged workers had 37% higher absenteeism, 49% more accidents, and 60% more errors and defects. In organizations with low employee engagement scores, they experienced 18% lower productivity, 16% lower profitability, 37% lower job growth, and 65% lower share price over time.[3]
- 69% of employees say they would work harder if they were appreciated.[4]

Accountability:[2]

- 72% believe leadership accountability is a critical business issue.
- 31% satisfied with the degree of leadership accountability.
- 49% have set clear leadership expectations.
- 45% demonstrate a high degree of commitment to their role as a leader.
- 20% have a strong leadership culture.
- 20% dare to address mediocre and unaccountable leaders.

The Meaning:

Many organizations tout their values on the websites, posters and speak to them. Do their actions match the values?

With values being at the very bottom of the Organizational Capability Map, they play the first, key part in the success of any organization's performance. Businesses select from hundreds of value words, and some may be different from the ones mentioned here. That is okay. Just note, the values I have selected here, are typically the root cause of most performance problems. And, when these values are not displayed at the very top, that behavior of your top leaders is what sets the tone for the rest of the organization. The values the organization displays is the foundation to "the culture" (the business performance foundation) or the "how" we deliver our business. They are your beliefs or guiding principles that every person in your organization lives. They are the true North of your moral compass.

The key values I have selected for this book are:

- Trust/Integrity/Honesty - Operating daily where your thoughts, words, and actions are all congruent. But this value is not mutually exclusive from other values such as Respect. Someone who is rude or hurtful to others can say, "Well, I was only being honest and transparent."
- Respect - Some may say, treat others as you expect to be treated. Be careful with that. Some people behave very badly and think it's okay. Respect, defined here is as follows: to appreciate the abilities, qualities, and attributes that make up any person, place, or thing.
- Passion/Purpose -This could also mean drive (see Daniel Pink's book "Drive"). In the studies previously mentioned, indicate we are productive only three out of eight hours in our day. This is a loss of energy in our performance. The cost of that to an organization is daunting, as well as the cost of not doing anything about it. If you take a 1000-person company, averaging $100,000 salaries, working an average of 1840 hours per year (2080 - 4 weeks off) or 3/8 x 1840. That equals 640 productive hours per year,

or 1150 non-productive hours + 160 hours off per year = 1310 unproductive hours.
- Accountability – as a leader you are responsible to an employee to hold them accountable, give them the ability to do their job well and be successful. As a leader, you are also accountable for yourself, your actions and inactions.

What is it that people are doing for those other five hours per day? Meetings, chatting, complaining, day-dreaming, social media, or looking for another job. "Yes" to all those things, and when we are divorced from our purpose, we just wander about.

Examples:

Below are a few company examples of setbacks, success stories, and turnarounds where Values were mature or missing.

Company: Enron

The Setback: Enron was an American energy, commodities, and service company employing close to 20,000 people. In 2001, at its peak, Enron was valued at $90 billion and was the 7th largest company in the United States. When they went bankrupt in December 2001, shares previously worth $90.75 were trading at $0.26. Jobs were lost, investors' savings were gone, retiree futures were squandered, and even some lives were lost. In following years, it emerged that they creatively planned accounting fraud by shredding documents, starting partnerships with their own shell companies, and engaging in insider trading. Enron has become a well-known example of corporate corruption with a lack of moral values.

Company: DeLorean

The Setback: John DeLorean designed some prominent vehicles throughout his career, including the Pontiac GTO, Firebird, and Grand Prix. In 1973, DeLorean started his own company and began working on a new prototype made with stainless steel, sleek lines, and doors that opened vertically. His DeLorean sports car hit the streets in 1980. Over the next three years, only 8,900 cars would be made. The car played a feature role in the film "Back to the Future" and became an American status symbol. Then, in 1982, DeLorean was charged with trafficking cocaine following a sting operation, later to be acquitted on entrapment grounds and cleared of defrauding his partners. DeLorean's reputation and company, however, were ruined.

Company: British Petroleum's Oil Spill

The Setback: Following the BP oil spill incident in 2010, they aired some expensive commercials apologizing for their actions. It turned out to be too much, though, and the public deemed it disingenuous. They even received criticism from President Obama and others, who said the money they put into the ads should have been invested in cleaning up the mess. Tony Hayward, CEO of BP, also made the fatal mistake of saying, "I'd like my life back," which showed a complete lack of respect for those who had actually lost their lives in the explosion.[5]

Values: What's the Diagnosis?

Symptoms:

This could be the most painful or gratifying chapter you read. Either way, I placed it here so it would be your final lesson in the book. Symptoms of bad values in an organization rear their ugly head in so many ways. Consciously or unconsciously, every single person emulates their values daily. Our values are built from our experiences growing up during our formative years with our parents, siblings, peers, school, community, television characters, books, and work. It is this culmination of all these experiences by which you measure yourself and others.

Here are what a few symptoms might look like from the inside of an organization:

Distrust/Lack of Trust, Integrity, or Honesty:

1. Withholding of information.
2. Micro-management. This may look like someone who doesn't trust their abilities to lead and will overcompensate or, they don't trust their employees enough to be successful so the manager will micro-manage their employees to do and say exactly as they would themselves.
3. Inconsistency between actions and words.
4. Changing of minds and opinions or the change in loyalty.
5. People who focus on making the most important person happy (unless it's your wife of course).
6. Working in silos.
7. Exclusion is used more than inclusion.

Lack of Respect

1. Rejecting thoughts and ideas.
2. Ignoring employees.
3. Breaking boundaries.
4. Violating trust.
5. Taking credit where credit is not deserved.

6. Rumors.
7. Derogatory comments.
8. Facial gestures of disgust, sneering.
9. Inattention during a conversation.
10. Lack of Empathy.
11. Sexual harassment.

Lack of Passion/Purpose:

1. Decreased productivity.
2. Employees don't speak up when things go wrong.
3. Lack of progress.
4. Passing the buck, scapegoats, finger-pointing.
5. Employees are complaining about how busy they are instead of getting the work done.
6. Lack of learning.
7. Micro-management.
8. Job insecurity.
9. Lack of confidence in organizational leadership.
10. Refer to the organization as "they."
11. The car park is empty fairly early in the day, consistently.
12. Employees are shut down in meetings or leaders do all the talking.
13. Visually, people don't look happy. There is a lack of laughter.

Lack of Accountability:

1. Displaying indifference, or not being definitive, not having an opinion or making a decision.
2. Missed deadlines.
3. Repeated mistakes.
4. Variability in quality output.
5. The presence of non-performers that are not managed.
6. Bad behaviors not managed.
7. Lots of babysitting of able adults.
8. A higher focus on employees keeping their jobs vs. doing their jobs.
9. Passing the buck, scapegoats, finger-pointing.

10. Inattention to detail.
11. Attrition of high performers.
12. Political talent management or the promotion of weak/ineffective leaders.
13. Not showing up to work.
14. Bullies exist.
15. False consensus in meetings.

This is how a negative set of values looks from the outside in:

1. Not following up on customer commitments.
2. Blaming the customer.
3. The office is a mess.
4. Only managers have offices.
5. The organization doesn't talk about their values to potential hires or their customers.
6. Employees refer to the company as "they" instead of "we."
7. Glassdoor does not look good and, if it is, feedback from anonymous-current employees is even worse. Many employers will discount or not even review the feedback on Glassdoor. Some will say, "they were disgruntled when they left." That situation does happen. My suggestion is to review the total set of feedback. What is the overall approval rating of the CEO? What does the feedback say about the leadership? Is there a consistent theme?
8. When you are inside the organization or meet any of the employees, you can't get a feel for the brand.

At Palentine, one of the leaders and I were having a one-on-one to discuss a critical project. Progress was slow with the implementation team due to the downsizing of a large number of employees with product domain expertise. The theory was that employees would be let go in specific areas of the company to hire a 3rd party provider that would create the product.

This leader expected the team to fill in the extra time the missing domain expertise would have provided to get the project completed. I remember the conversation well as it was Christmas time and we were discussing the request to allow the team to use their holiday time that had been originally planned before the downsizing.

The leader looked at me and said, "You mid-westerners are all too nice, who gives a crap about Christmas." While I work on a solution, this response made it difficult when he clearly did not respect the employees, their families, or the Values of the company.

Value Examples:

Some of these examples below are from long-standing organizations with, as I have defined in this book, a mix of values and organizational capabilities:

- **Accenture:** Stewardship: The Best People: Client Value Creation: One Global Network: *Respect* for the Individual: *Integrity*
- **American Express:** Customer Commitment: Quality: *Integrity*: Teamwork (I have called this Collaboration in this book): *Respect* for People: Good Citizenship: A Will to Win: Personal *Accountability*
- **Coca-Cola:** Leadership: Collaboration: *Integrity*: *Accountability*: *Passion*: Diversity: Quality
- **Procter & Gamble:** *Integrity*: Leadership: Ownership: *Passion* for Winning: Trust
- **Kellogg:** *Integrity*: *Accountability*: *Passion*: Humility: Simplicity: Results

The Assessment:

Evaluate the symptoms previously mentioned. If a large portion of your organization exhibits these behaviors, it is a systemic problem that will show itself through the speed at which you deliver, the quality of your product and services, how satisfied your customers are, and so on. The values you choose to display for your organization are the foundation to everything you do. I have selected the values: accountability, respect, passion, and trust because they are typically just expected out of employees and are common amongst a large number of companies.

Baseline Your Maturity Level:

Level 1: Broken:

Your culture is broken. You found at least ten of the above symptoms were true and fairly symptomatic. You stopped counting, and your head is now in your hands.

Level 3: Continuously Improving:

You may have found one or two of episodic symptoms above, that with some attention can be easily resolved in a few months.

Level 5: A Stable Protective Foundation:

You got it. These symptoms don't exist in your company. Your employees live and breathe the company values.

Your baseline maturity level for Values is: _____

Values: Mind the Gap

After diagnosing where you are with your value levels, the next steps are as follows:

Level 1: Broken:

1. Re-evaluate your organization's values, mission, and vision.
2. Start modeling the values at the top levels of leadership in your organization.
3. Communicate the expectations.
4. Publicize and incentivize the display of the values you want to be emulated.
5. Focus on the positive impact of the behavior changes.

Level 3: Continuously Improving:

1. Evaluate value performance.
2. Manage episodic performance.

Level 5: A Stable Protective Foundation:

1. Protect it. Whatever you are doing, keep doing it.
2. Watch the heartbeat of your culture closely.

Chapter 20

Don't Let Your Culture Eat Your Strategy For Lunch!

You've done it. After reading about each of the Organizational Capabilities, you should have taken a look at your Vision, Mission, and Goals, and identified what Capability was most critical? Then you took a look at what your customers expect most from what your business offers. Was it quality or maybe customer service? Then take a look at the process and people capabilities you need to deliver on your Vision, Mission, Goals and customer expectations. What was your list?

I also mentioned there are three that you need to mature and excel at first; then the rest will come easier and faster. Fail at these three, and your efforts will be costly. Those first three are Values, Leadership, and Talent. Did they make your list? Are they the top priority?

Write your capabilities down here for future reference, in priority order including your baseline score.

Capability	Baseline Score	Priority
Strategic Focus		
Leadership		
Talent		
Domain Expertise		
Productivity		
Continuous Learning		
Innovation		
Brand Identity		
Collaboration		
Customer Intimacy		
Customer Service		
Speed & Agility		
Quality		

Capability	Baseline Score	Priority
Enabling Technology		
Strategic Partnerships		
Effective Communication		
Values		

Summing It All Up

So, let's revisit a few of the statistics we saw previously. If you are plagued with a lack of maturity in your organizational capabilities, how much profit are you really making?

- What is the cost of disengaged employees to you?
- What is the cost of the lack of productivity (62% not productive or 3 out of 8 hours is productivity)?
- What is the cost of poor communication in your company (15%)?
- What is the cost of poor quality for you (15–40%)?
- And, what is the cost of poor customer service for you?

With incremental investments in your organizational capabilities, how much could you move to the bottom line to re-invest or share in the profits? How much happier would your customers be? How much more would your company be worth to a buyer? How much longer would you increase the tenure of your company?

Honestly, the road ahead to change your culture and build these capabilities could be long and possibly difficult. But, once you start, your organization will respond and the speed at which you improve will increase. But, getting started is the key. Have the courage to start and continuously move forward, and as you "Mind The Gap" you will be building a foundation for the future that will enable your organization to unleash its limitless business performance.

References and Other Related Resources

Introduction:

Sources:

1. Crabtree, Steve. "Worldwide, 13% of Employees are Engaged at Work." *Gallup News*. 8 October 2013. http://news.gallup.com/poll/165269/worldwide-employees-engaged-work.aspx
2. Curtin, Melanie. "In an 8-Hour Day, the Average Worker is Productive for This Many Hours." *Inc.* 21 Jul 2016. https://www.inc.com/melanie-curtin/in-an-8-hour-day-the-average-worker-is-productive-for-this-many-hours.html
3. Wagner, Eric. "Five Reasons 8 Out of 10 Businesses Fail" *Forbes*. 12 September 2013. https://www.forbes.com/sites/ericwagner/2013/09/12/five-reasons-8-out-of-10-businesses-fail/#6978dfe76978
4. Prosser, Dan. "Are You a Thirteener? Why Only 13 Percent of Companies Successfully Execute Their Strategies." *Young Up Starts*. 9 March 2015 http://www.youngupstarts.com/2015/03/09/why-only-13-percent-of-companies-successfully-execute-their-strategies/
5. Neville, Betsy & Benedict, Neil. "Strategic Initiatives Study: Adapting Corporate Strategy to the Changing Economy." FD | *Forbes Insights*. 9 January 2018. https://i.forbesimg.com/forbesinsights/StudyPDFs/FD_AdaptingCorporateStrategy.pdf
6. Leinwand, Paul, Mainardi, Cesare, & Kleiner, Art. "Only 8% of Leaders Are Good at Both Strategy and Execution." *HBR*. 30 December 2015. https://hbr.org/2015/12/only-8-of-leaders-are-good-at-both-strategy-and-execution
7. Transformative Work Design. "A Future That Works: Automation, Employment and Productivity." *McKinsey Global Instituate*. October 2016. https://www.transformativeworkdesign.com/single-post/2017/04/19/McKinsey-Co-Report-on-future-work-and-the-impact-on-global-productivity
8. Consultant's Mind. "How Big is the Gig Economy?" *Consultant's Mind*. 31 October 2016. http://www.consultantsmind.com/2016/10/31/gig-economy/
9. Gallap. "Dismal Employee Engagement Is a Sign of Global Mismanagement." Gallop News. 20 December 2017. http://news.gallup.com/opinion/gallup/224012/dismal-employee-engagement-sign-global-mismanagement.aspx

Chapter 3: Strategic Focus

Sources:

1. McKinsey&Company. "Ascending to the C-suite." *McKinsey.com*. April 2015. http://www.mckinsey.com/global-themes/leadership/ascending-to-the-c-suite
2. Leinwand, Paul, Mainardi, Cesare, & Kleiner, Art. "Only 8% of Leaders Are Good at Both Strategy and Execution." HBR. 30 December 2015. https://hbr.org/2015/12/only-8-of-leaders-are-good-at-both-strategy-and-execution
3. Neville, Betsy & Benedict, Neil. "Strategic Initiatives Study: Adapting Corporate Strategy to the Changing Economy." FD | *Forbes Insights*. 9 January 2018. https://i.forbesimg.com/forbesinsights/StudyPDFs/FD_AdaptingCorporateStrategy.pdf
4. Pierce, Jack. "Three Reasons Why Good Strategies Fail: Execution, Execution..." *Knowledge@Wharton*. 10 August 2005. http://knowledge.wharton.upenn.edu/article/three-reasons-why-good-strategies-fail-execution-execution/
5. Prosser, Dan. "Are You a Thirteener? Why Only 13 Percent of Companies Successfully Execute Their Strategies." Young Up Starts. 9 March 2015 http://www.youngupstarts.com/2015/03/09/why-only-13-percent-of-companies-successfully-execute-their-strategies/
6. Caldbeck, Ryan. "Why Execution Is Everything in Business." *Forbes*. 16 September 2014. https://www.forbes.com/sites/ryancaldbeck/2014/09/16/why-execution-is-everything/#32753769777b
7. Levy, Adam. "Blue Apron's Failed Execution Just Opened the Door for the Competition." The Motley Fool. 15 August 2017. https://www.fool.com/investing/2017/08/15/blue-aprons-failed-execution-just-opened-the-door.aspx
8. Spors, Kelly K. "9 Business Icons Who Faced Utter Failure and Came Back to Kick Arse." Business Insider Australia. 13 April 2011. https://www.businessinsider.com.au/famous-business-failures-and-comebacks-2011-4#henry-ford-1863-1947-1

Related Resources:

1. Zwilling, Martin. "6 Ways That Lack of Focus Can Kill Your Business." *Forbes*. 16 December 2014. https://www.forbes.com/sites/martinzwilling/2014/12/16/6-ways-that-lack-of-focus-can-kill-your-business/#497c2cce1a21
2. Lazazzera, Richard. "The Importance of Focus for Your Ecommerce Business and How to Achieve It." *Shopify*. 10 February 2015. https://www.

shopify.com/blog/17113712-the-importance-of-focus-for-your-ecommerce-business-and-how-to-achieve-it

3. Stark, Karl & Stewart, Bill. "How to Capitalize on Your Lack of Focus." *Inc.* 26 March 2012. https://www.inc.com/karl-and-bill/how-to-capitalize-on-your-lack-of-focus.html

4. Aileron. "10 Reasons Why Strategic Plans Fail." *Forbes*. 30 November 2011. https://www.forbes.com/sites/aileron/2011/11/30/10-reasons-why-strategic-plans-fail/#548d5e7f86a8

5. Aileron. "Five Steps to a Strategic Plan." *Forbes*. 25 October 2011. https://www.forbes.com/sites/aileron/2011/10/25/five-steps-to-a-strategic-plan/#5de57dd35464

6. Inc. Staff. "The 5 Habits of Quality-Focused Companies." Inc. 31 January 2011. https://www.inc.com/guides/201101/five-habits-of-quality-focused-companies.html

Chapter 4: Leadership

Sources:

1. Markway, Barbara. "The Heart of Effective Leadership." *Psychology Today*. 21 January 2015. https://www.psychologytoday.com/blog/living-the-questions/201501/the-heart-effective-leadership
2. Loew, Laci. "Study Shows Leadership Development Rated Below Average or Poor in More Than One-Third of Organizations." *Training Magazine*. 28 May 2015. https://trainingmag.com/study-shows-leadership-development-rated-below-average-or-poor-more-one-third-organizations
3. Smykal, Emily. "8 Stats on Millennials and Leadership in the Workplace." *Jibe*. 26 August 2015. https://www.jibe.com/blog/8-stats-on-millennials-and-leadership-in-the-workplace/
4. Wilcox, Laura. "Emotional Intelligence is no Soft Skill." *Harvard University Blog*. 9 January 2018. https://www.extension.harvard.edu/professional-development/blog/emotional-intelligence-no-soft-skill
5. Goleman, Daniel. "Leadership That Gets Results." *HBR*. March-April 2000. https://hbr.org/2000/03/leadership-that-gets-results
6. Bersin, Josh. "Why Companies Fail to Engage Today's Workforce: The Overwhelmed Employee." Forbes. 15 March 2014. https://www.forbes.com/sites/joshbersin/2014/03/15/why-companies-fail-to-engage-todays-workforce-the-overwhelmed-employee/#159e4d354726
7. Chamorro-Premuzic, Tomas & Murphy, Clarke. "When Leaders Are Hired for Talent but Fired for Not Fitting In." *HBR*. 14 June 2017. https://hbr.org/2017/06/when-leaders-are-hired-for-talent-but-fired-for-not-fitting-in
8. "World's Greatest Leaders." *Fortune*. 2017. http://fortune.com/worlds-greatest-leaders/

Related Resources:

1. Service Leadership. "The What and Why of Operational Maturity Levels: Enabling the Measurement and Comparison of Profitability and Best Practices." *Service Leadership*. 9 January 2018. http://www.service-leadership.com/assets/pdf/The_What_and_Why_of_Operational_Maturity_Levels(c)-2016-Service-Leadership.pdf
2. Benincasa, Robyn. "6 Leadership Styles and When You Should Use Them." *Fast Company*. 29 May 2012. https://www.fastcompany.com/1838481/6-leadership-styles-and-when-you-should-use-them

3   Management Study Guide Content Team. "Level 5 Leadership." *MSG.* 9 January 2018. http://www.managementstudyguide.com/level-5-leadership.htm
4   Myatt, Mike. "15 Ways to Identify Bad Leaders." *Forbes.* 18 October 2012. https://www.forbes.com/sites/mikemyatt/2012/10/18/15-ways-to-identify-bad-leaders/#5caea63515da
5   Cravenho, Andrew. "7 Ways to Identify Leaders Among Your Employees." *Fast Company.* 20 April 2015. https://www.fastcompany.com/3044953/7-ways-to-identify-leaders-among-your-employees
6   Javitsh, Dr. David G. "10 Qualities of Superior Leaders." *Entrepreneur.* 9 December 2009. https://www.entrepreneur.com/article/204248#
7   Maxwell, John C. "Leadership Gold: Lessons I've Learned from a Lifetime of Leading".

Chapter 5: Talent

Sources:

1. Vaccaro, Alex. "The Talent Management Stats You Need to Know." *SABA*. 29 November 2016. https://www.saba.com/us/blogs/2016/11/29/talent-management-stats-you-need-to-know-saba/
2. Flade, Peter, Asplund, Jim & Elliot, Gwen. "Employees Who Use Their Strengths Outperform Those Who Don't." *Gallup News*. 8 October 2015. http://www.gallup.com/businessjournal/186044/employees-strengths-outperform-don.aspx
3. Bersin, Josh. "Why Companies Fail to Engage Today's Workforce: The Overwhelmed Employee. *Forbes*. 15 March 2014. https://www.forbes.com/sites/joshbersin/2014/03/15/why-companies-fail-to-engage-todays-workforce-the-overwhelmed-employee/#159e4d354726

Related Resources:

1. Sumtotal. "Using a Telent Mangement System to Give Your Company a Competitive Advantage." Sumtotal. 9 January 2018. http://learn.skillsoft.com/STS-Paid-Media-PPC-TalentManagement-Registration-Page.html
2. Heathfield, Susan M. "What Is Talent Management --Really?: Why Talent Management Is an Important Business Strategy to Develop." *The Balance*. 25 November 2017. https://www.thebalance.com/what-is-talent-management-really-1919221
3. "The Failure of Talent Identification." *Gartner*. 9 January 2018. https://www.cebglobal.com/insights/talent-assessment.html
4. Childers, Linda. "Get Better at Assessing Talent." *Monster*. 9 January 2018. https://hiring.monster.com/hr/hr-best-practices/small-business/hiring-process/assessing-talent.aspx

Chapter 6: Domain Expertise

Sources:

1. Wiseman, Liz. "Entrepreneurial Thought Leaders: Liz Wiseman of Multipliers and Rookie Smarts." *YouTube*. 4 Nov 2014. https://www.youtube.com/watch?v=RyJ6YRDTw20
2. MPS. "Why Do Products Fail?" *TheProduct.com*. 9 January 2018. http://www.theproduct.com/marketing/product_failure.htm
3. Turnaround. "Why Do Companies Fail? 2014 Survey Results." *TMS*. 10 February 2014. http://turnaround-society.com/companies-fail-2014-survey-results/

Related Resources:

1. Heathfield, Susan M. "What Is Talent Management --Really?: Why Talent Management Is an Important Business Strategy to Develop." *The Balance*. 25 November 2017. https://www.thebalance.com/what-is-talent-management-really-1919221
2. "The Failure of Talent Identification." *Gartner*. 9 January 2018. https://www.cebglobal.com/insights/talent-assessment.html
3. Childers, Linda. "Get Better at Assessing Talent." *Monster*. 9 January 2018. https://hiring.monster.com/hr/hr-best-practices/small-business/hiring-process/assessing-talent.aspx

Chapter 7: Productivity

Sources:

1   Mankins, Michael. "Great Companies Obsess Over Productivity, Not Efficiency." *HBR*. 1 March 2017. https://hbr.org/2017/03/great-companies-obsess-over-productivity-not-efficiency

Related Resources:

1   McFarlin, Kate. "The Effects of an Unproductive Workforce." *Chron*. 9 January 2018. http://smallbusiness.chron.com/effects-unproductive-workplace-10881.html
2   Andersen, Erika. "How to Make Your Employees As Unproductive As Possible." *Forbes*. 29 April 2013. https://www.forbes.com/sites/erikaandersen/2013/04/29/how-to-make-your-employees-as-unproductive-as-possible/#24c956951bb1
3   CMMI Product Team. "CMMI for Services, Version 1.3." *SEI*. November 2010. https://resources.sei.cmu.edu/library/asset-view.cfm?assetID=9665

Chapter 8: Continuous Learning

Sources:

1. Wadors, Pat. "To Stay Relevant, Your Company and Employees Must Keep Learning." *HBR*. 7 March 2016. https://hbr.org/2016/03/to-stay-relevant-your-company-and-employees-must-keep-learning
2. Cornelius, Kate. "Lifelong Learning: Why it's Critical for Today's Workforce." OpenSesame. 19 January 2015. https://www.opensesame.com/blog/lifelong-learning-why-its-critical-todays-workforce

Related Resources:

1. Wells, Joanne. "10 Ways to Build a Culture of Continuous Learning." *TD Magazine*. February 2017. https://www.td.org/magazines/td-magazine/10-ways-to-build-a-culture-of-continuous-learning
2. "How to Help Employees Embrace Continuous Learning." *Administrate*. 4 April 2014. https://www.getadministrate.com/blog/how-to-help-employees-embrace-continuous-learning/
3. Bersin, Josh. "5 Keys to Building a Learning Organization." *Forbes*. 18 January 2012. https://www.forbes.com/sites/joshbersin/2012/01/18/5-keys-to-building-a-learning-organization/#76aa555d129c
4. Ferrazzi, Keith. "7 Ways to Improve Employee Development Programs." *HBR*. 31 July 2015. https://hbr.org/2015/07/7-ways-to-improve-employee-development-programs
5. Amato, Mary Anne & Molokhia, Dalia. "How to Cultivate Learning Agility." Harvard Business Publishing. 9 January 2017. https://www.augusta.edu/leadershipacademy/white-papers/documents/learningagility.pdf
6. Bersin, Josh. "How Corporate Learning Drives Competitive Advantage." *Forbes*. 20 March 2013. https://www.forbes.com/sites/joshbersin/2013/03/20/how-corporate-learning-drives-competitive-advantage/#3f6b26e017ad
7. Gino, Francesca & Staats, Bradly. "Why Organizations Don't Learn." *HBR*. November 2015. https://hbr.org/2015/11/why-organizations-dont-learn
8. Gino Francesca & Pisano Gary P. "Why Leaders Don't Learn from Success." *HBR*. April 2011. https://hbr.org/2011/04/why-leaders-dont-learn-from-success

Chapter 9: Innovation

Sources:

1. Denning, Steve. "Why U.S. Firms Are Dying: Failure to Innovate." *Forbes*. 27 February 2015. https://www.forbes.com/sites/stevedenning/2015/02/27/is-there-an-innovation-crisis-at-us-firms/#2dbf0ba164cb
2. Vocoli. "10 Companies That Failed to Innovate and What Happened to Them." *Vocoli Blog*. 21 July 2014. https://www.vocoli.com/blog/july-2014/10-companies-that-failed-to-innovate-and-what-happened-to-them/
3. Claveria, Kelvin. "13 Stunning Stats About Product Innovation." *VisionCritical*. 15 April 2016. https://www.visioncritical.com/stats-product-innovation/

Related Resources:

1. Fenn, Jackie & Harris, Kathy. "A Maturity Model for Innovation Management. *Gartner*. 16 August 2017. https://www.gartner.com/doc/1621015/maturity-model-innovation-management
2. Kelley, Braden. "Measuring Your Innovation Maturity." *Innovation Excellence*. 9 January 2018. http://innovationexcellence.com/blog/2017/04/27/measuring-your-innovation-maturity/
3. Wirkus, Craig. "Building the Right Innovation Maturity Model for your Business." *Cisco Blogs*. 5 October 2017. https://blogs.cisco.com/innovation/building-the-right-innovation-maturity-model-for-your-business
4. Nauyalis, Carrie. "A New Framework for Assessing Your Innovation Program." Planview. 9 January 2018. http://www2.planview.com/im3/docs/Planview-Innovation-Maturity-Model.pdf

Chapter 10: Brand Identity

Sources:

1. Hammis, Eric. "How Important Is Brand Identity?" Business 2 Community. 2 April 2015. Infohttp://www.business2community.com/infographics/important-brand-identity-infographic-01197538#8EWHAkQuAk4bGmdS.97

Related Resources:

1. Fitzgerald, Caitlin. "Five Ways to Avoid Brand Failure." *Prae*. 22 August 2017. https://www.praeagency.com/blog/five-ways-to-avoid-brand-failure
2. Male, Bianca. "10 Major Rebranding Disasters and What You Should Learn From Them." *Business Insider*. 7 April 2010. http://www.businessinsider.com/rebranding-failures-2010-3
3. Daye, Derrick. "41 Causes of Brand Failure." *Branding Strategy Insider*. 21 October 2010. https://www.brandingstrategyinsider.com/2010/10/41-causes-of-brand-failure.html#.Wi_t-LQ-e3c
4. Lischer, Brian. "Six Reasons Your Company May Need to Rebrand Itself." *Forbes*. 21 October 2016. https://www.forbes.com/sites/theyec/2016/10/21/six-reasons-your-company-may-need-to-rebrand-itself/#47cbd683770e

Chapter 11: Collaboration

Sources:

1. Marketwire. "New Study: 86 Percent of Employees Cite Lack of Collaboration for Workplace Failures." Yahoo. 23 May 2011. https://www.yahoo.com/news/New-Study-86-Percent-of-iw-1701397200.html
2. Globe Newswire. "Businesses Lose an Average of $11,000 per Employee Every Year Due to Ineffective Communications and Collaboration." Mitel Newsroom. 23 March 2017. http://www.mitel.com/newsroom/news-releases/businesses-lose-average-11000-employee-every-year-due-ineffective

Related Resources:

1. Morgan, Jacob. "The 12 Habits of Highly Collaborative Organizations." *Forbes*. 30 July 2013. https://www.forbes.com/sites/jacobmorgan/2013/07/30/the-12-habits-of-highly-collaborative-organizations/#42245bf53683
2. Doyle, Alison. "Collaboration Definition, Skills, and Examples." *The Balance*. 11 March 2017. https://www.thebalance.com/collaboration-skills-with-examples-2059686
3. Krigsman, Michael. "CIO View: Ten Principles for Effective Collaboration." *ZDNet*. 6 September 2011. http://www.zdnet.com/article/cio-view-ten-principles-for-effective-collaboration/
4. Daum, Kevin. "How Smart People Collaborate for Success." *Inc*. 21 June 2013. https://www.inc.com/kevin-daum/how-smart-people-collaborate-for-success.html
5. Tyson, Bruce. "Characteristics of Effective Collaboration." *Bright Hub Project Management*. 19 May 2011. http://www.brighthubpm.com/resource-management/70714-characteristics-of-effective-collaboration/
6. McQuerrey, Lisa. "Examples of Poor Teamwork." *Career Trend*. 5 July 2017. https://careertrend.com/examples-poor-teamwork-12860.html
7. Rosenthal, Beth & Mizrahi, Terry. "Strategic Partnerships: How to Crete and Maintain Interorganizational Collaborations and Coalitions." *Hunter College*. 9 January 2018. http://www.hunter.cuny.edu/socwork/ecco/strategic_partnerships.htm and http://www.hunter.cuny.edu/socwork/ecco/coalition_project/j.htm
8. Goman, Dr. Carol Kinsey. "7 Insights for Collaboration in the Workplace." *Reliable Plant*. 9 January 2018. http://www.reliableplant.com/Read/23929/7-insights-collaboration-workplace
9. Cooperrider, David. "What Is Appreciative Inquiry?" *David Cooperrider & Associates*. 9 January 2018. http://www.davidcooperrider.com/ai-process/

Chapter 12: Customer Intimacy

Sources:

1. Davies, Simon. "Customer Intimacy - A Strategic Choice - Not the Same as 'Customer Focused.'" *On The Mark*. 8 January 2011. https://on-the-mark.com/customer-intimacy-a-strategic-choice-not-the-same-as-customer-focused/
2. Lyon, Ethan. "Mercedes Gets Profitable Through Customer Intimacy." *Sparxoo*. 9 January 2018. http://sparxoo.com/2010/07/06/mercedes-gets-profitable-through-customer-intimacy/
3. Power, Brad. "Operational Excellence, Meet Customer Intimacy." *HBR*. 29 March 2013. https://hbr.org/2013/03/operational-excellence-meet-cu
4. Conlon, Ginger. "Are You Really Ready for Customer Experience?" *DMN*. 10 October 2014. http://www.dmnews.com/marketing-strategy/are-you-really-ready-for-customer-experience/article/376573/
5. CMG. "3 Easy Steps to More Effective Customer Engagement." *CMG*. 9 January 2018. http://cmgpartners.com/content/customer-engagement/
6. Kalra, Ashish. "Why Customers Quit?" *LinkedIn Pulse*. 27 February 2015. https://www.linkedin.com/pulse/why-customers-quit-ashish-kalra

Related Resources:

1. Weinman, Joe. "How Customer Intimacy is Evolving to Collective Intimacy, Thanks to Big Data." *Forbes*. 4 June 2013. https://www.forbes.com/sites/joeweinman/2013/06/04/how-customer-intimacy-is-evolving-to-collective-intimacy-thanks-to-big-data/#297c092f5dbc
2. Kaput, Michael Batton. "How to Restructure to Build Intimacy With Customers." *Chron*. 9 January 2018. http://smallbusiness.chron.com/restructure-build-intimacy-customers-21242.html
3. CMG. "6 Most Effective Customer Intimacy Strategies." *CMG*. 9 January 2018. http://cmgpartners.com/content/customer-intimacy-strategy/
4. Olsen, Erica. "Strategic Planning: Leading With Customer Intimacy." *Dummies*. 9 January 2018. http://www.dummies.com/business/business-strategy/strategic-planning-leading-with-customer-intimacy/

Chapter 13: Customer Service

Sources:

1. States, Kim. "Three Businesses That Failed for Lack of Customer Service." *Inside Tucson Business*. 2 September 2011. http://www.insidetucsonbusiness.com/news/on_guard/three-businesses-that-failed-for-lack-of-customer-service/article_42816a5e-d4df-11e0-9b64-001cc4c002e0.html
2. Help Scout. "75 Customer Service Facts, Quotes, & Statistics. The Cost of Bad Customer Service." *Help Scout*. 9 January 2018. https://www.helpscout.net/75-customer-service-facts-quotes-statistics/
3. Hyken, Shep. "Ten Customer Service and Customer Experience Trends for 2017." *Forbes*. 7 January 2017. https://www.forbes.com/sites/shephyken/2017/01/07/10-customer-service-and-customer-experience-cx-trends-for-2017/#1fa3cf2175e5
4. Zendesk. "What is Bad Customer Service?" *Zendesk Library*. 9 January 2018. https://www.zendesk.com/resources/what-is-bad-customer-service/
5. Knufken, Drea. "The 25 Worst Business Failures in History." *Business Pundit*. 14 January 2009. http://www.businesspundit.com/the-25-worst-business-failures-in-history/

Related Resources:

1. The Institute of Customer Service. "Setting Customer Service Standards." *The Institute of Customer Service Research & Insight*. 8 June 2015. https://www.instituteofcustomerservice.com/research-insight/guidance-notes/article/setting-customer-service-standards
2. Swincoe, Adrian. "How to Implement An Effective Proactive Customer Service Strategy." *Forbes*. 2 February 2015. https://www.forbes.com/sites/adrianswinscoe/2015/02/02/how-to-implement-an-effective-proactive-customer-service-strategy/#4a641482650e
3. Callinan, Lisa, Coppinger, Beth, Poole, Chris. "Use Gartner's Maturity Model to Improve Customer Service." *Gartner*. 20 March 2017. https://www.gartner.com/doc/3645319/use-gartners-maturity-model-improve.

Chapter 14: Speed and Agility

Sources:

1. Bazigos, Michael, de Smet, Aaron, & Gagnon, Chris. "Why Agility Pays." *McKinsey Quarterly*. December 2015. https://www.mckinsey.com/business-functions/organization/our-insights/why-agility-pays
2. Sull, Donald. "Cometing Through Organizational Agility." *McKinsey Quarterly*. December 2009. https://www.mckinsey.com/business-functions/organization/our-insights/competing-through-organizational-agility

Related Resources:

1. Walker, Susan. "5 Most Important Business Agility Traits." *D!gitalist Magazine*. 5 August 2015. http://www.digitalistmag.com/digital-economy/2015/08/05/top-5-business-agility-traits-03249545
2. Economy, Peter. "8 Powerful Ways to Build a Faster, More Agile Business." Inc. 10 December 2014. https://www.inc.com/peter-economy/8-powerful-ways-to-build-a-faster-more-agile-business.html
3. Gothelf, Jeff. "Bring Agile to the Whole Organization." HBR. 14 November 2014. https://hbr.org/2014/11/bring-agile-to-the-whole-organization

Chapter 15: Quality

Sources:

1. The Quality Portal. "Cost of Quality: Overview." *The Quality Portal.* 9 January 2018. http://thequalityportal.com/q_CoQ.htm
2. Matteson, Michael & Metivier, Chris. "Business Ethics - Case: The Ford Pinto." *Philosophia.* 9 January 2018. https://philosophia.uncg.edu/phi361-matteson/module-1-why-does-business-need-ethics/case-the-ford-pinto/
3. Kelly, Jeff. "Poor Data Quality Costing Companies Millions of Dollars Annually." *Search Data Management.* 25 Aug 2009. http://searchdatamanagement.techtarget.com/news/1365965/Poor-data-quality-costing-companies-millions-of-dollars-annually

Related Resources:

1. MetricStream. "9 Key Strategies to Minimize the Cost of Poor Quality." MetricStream Resources/Insights. 9 January 2018. https://www.metricstream.com/insights/costofPoorQuality_home.htm
2. Inc. Staff. "5 Ways to Improve Quality." Inc. 9 January 2018. https://www.inc.com/guides/2010/09/5-ways-to-improve-quality.html
3. Project Management Hacks Team. "4 Ways to Improve Quality." *Project Management Hacks.* 9 January 2018. http://projectmanagementhacks.com/improve-quality/

Chapter 16: Enabling Technology

Sources:

1. Morgan, Steve. "Is Poor Software Development the Biggest Cyber Threat." *CSO*. 2 September 2015. https://www.csoonline.com/article/2978858/application-security/is-poor-software-development-the-biggest-cyber-threat.html
2. Campbell, Anita. "The Top 3 Reasons to Implement Restaurant Technology." *Small Business Trends*. 26 May 2016. https://smallbiztrends.com/2016/05/implement-restaurant-technology.html
3. Fisher, Sharon. "Schools Turn to Technology to Save Money." 19 May 2014. Simplicity 2.0. https://www.laserfiche.com/simplicity/schools-turn-technology-save-money/
4. IT Trends Study Research Team. "Issues, Investments, Concerns, & Practices of Organizations and Their IT Executives: Results and Observations from the 2018 SIM IT Trends Study." *Society of Information Management*. November 2018. p 25.

Related Resources:

1. Staff Contributors. "12 Ways to Leverage Technology to Improve Business Productivity." *YFS Magazine*. 10 May 2013. http://yfsmagazine.com/2013/05/10/12-ways-to-leverage-technology-to-improve-business-productivity/2/
2. Xantrion. "How to Leverage Information Technology to Develop a Competitive Advantage. *Xantrion Articles*. 9 January 2018. https://www.xantrion.com/article/how-to-leverage-information-technology-to-develop-a-competitive-advantage
3. Porter, Micheal E. and Millar, Victor E. "How Information Gives You a Competitive Advantage. *HBR*. July 1985. https://hbr.org/1985/07/how-information-gives-you-competitive-advantage

Chapter 17: Strategic Partnerships

Sources:

1. Lie, Eunje. "10 Business Partnerships That Went Down in Flames." *Business Insider*. 23 November 2010. http://www.businessinsider.com/11-excruciating-business-partner-breakups-2010-11?op=1

Related Resources:

1. Brown, Carolyn M. "13 Facets of an Effective Business Partnership." *Black Enterprise*. 15 July 2014. http://www.blackenterprise.com/13-facets-an-effective-business-partnership/
2. Elsner, Michael D. "'Working Together': Why Successful Business Partnerships Are As Important As Successful Marriages." *Huffpost*. 14 September 2010. https://www.huffingtonpost.com/michael-d-eisner/business-partnerships-marriage_b_715237.html
3. Spence, John. "Strategic Partnerships as Effective Business Growth Strategies." *John Spence Blog*. 29 October 2015. http://blog.johnspence.com/2015/10/strategic-partnerships-effective-business-growth-strategies/
4. Neville, Amanda. "5 Signs Your Partnership is Doomed." *Forbes*. 15 March 2013. https://www.forbes.com/sites/amandaneville/2013/03/15/5-signs-your-partnership-is-doomed/#7bf6b1dac826
5. Useem, Andrea. "5 Keys to Effective Partnerships." *DevEx*. 5 November 2012. https://www.devex.com/news/5-keys-to-effective-partnerships-79643

Chapter 18: Effective Communication

Sources:

1. Burke, Kenneth. "24 Business Communication Statistics That Prove You Should Be Texting." *Text Request*. 10 November 2015. https://www.textrequest.com/blog/24-statistics-that-prove-texting-is-the-largest-void-in-business-communication/
2. Paton, Cassie. "7 Surprising Stats That Show the Importance of Internal Communications." *Enplug Blog*. 13 May 2015. https://blog.enplug.com/7-surprising-internal-communications-stats
3. Pollock, Sara. "Final Destination: Organizational Transparency." *ClearCompany*. 9 January 2016. https://blog.clearcompany.com/final-destination-organizational-transparency
4. Mital. "Businesses Lose an Average of $11,000 per Employee Every Year Due to Ineffective Communications and Collaboration." *Mitel Newsroom*. 23 March 2017. http://www.mitel.com/newsroom/news-releases/businesses-lose-average-11000-employee-every-year-due-ineffective
5. Groysberg, Boris and Slind, Michael. "The Silent Killer of Big Companies." *HBR*. 25 October 2012. https://hbr.org/2012/10/the-silent-killer-of-big-companies
6. Phillips, Harry. "Don't Faill Into The 'I Failed To Communicate.' Trap." *LinkedIn Pulse*. 11 October 2015. https://www.linkedin.com/pulse/dont-fall-i-failed-communicate-trap-harry-phillips

Related Resources:

1. Minto, Barbara. "The Minto Pyramid Principle." 9 January 2018. http://www.barbaraminto.com/
2. Institute for Health and Human Potential. "Science of Emotional Intelligence." 9 January 2018. https://www.ihhp.com/emotional-intelligence-training/#accordion_12854846512
3. Psychology Today. "Emotional Intelligence Test". 9 January 2018. https://www.psychologytoday.com/tests/personality/emotional-intelligence-test
4. IESE Business School. "Why You Need Cultural Intelligence (And How To Develop It)." *Forbes*. 24 March 2015. https://www.forbes.com/sites/iese/2015/03/24/why-you-need-cultural-intelligence-and-how-to-develop-it/#13b617f17d68

Chapter 19: Values

Sources:

1. Douglas, Eric. "New Research Underscores the Importance of Trust." *Leading Resources Incorporated.* 19 April 2017. https://leading-resources.com/leadership/new-research-underscores-the-importance-of-trust/
2. Molinaro, Vince. "The Leadership Accountability Gap." *LHH.* 10 May 2017. https://www.lhh.com/our-knowledge/2017/the-leadership-accountability-gap
3. Seppala, Emma and Cameron, Kim. "Proor That Postive Work Cultures Are More Productive." *HBR.* 01 December 2015. https://hbr.org/2015/12/proof-that-positive-work-cultures-are-more-productive
4. Paton, Cassie. "7 Surprising Stats That Show the Importance of Internal Communications." *Enplug Blog.* 13 May 2015. https://blog.enplug.com/7-surprising-internal-communications-stats
5. Grasshopper Team. "8 Epic Communication Failures." *Grasshopper Blog.* 7 June 2011. https://grasshopper.com/blog/8-epic-failures-of-communication/

Related Resources:

1. Ross, Marie-Claire. "5 Signs of a Dysfunctional Culture". *Cascade.* 1 April 2016. https://www.executestrategy.net/blog/5-signs-dysfunctional-culture/
2. Burke, Adrienne. "Five signs you are in a toxic office. *Yahoo Small Business.* 8 January 2018. https://smallbusiness.yahoo.com/advisor/blogs/profit-minded/five-signs-office-culture-terrible-164034898.html
3. Ryan, Liz. "Ten Unmistakable Signs Of A Toxic Culture." *Forbes.* 19 October 2016. https://www.forbes.com/sites/lizryan/2016/10/19/ten-unmistakable-signs-of-a-toxic-culture/#4a6d4ff115fe
4. Pink, Daniel H. *"Drive: The Surprising Truth About What Motivates Us".* 5 April 2011.

About the Author

Kimberle Seale

Kimberle Seale, President of Vincerem and MTG Press, is an experienced corporate executive with an extensive background in strategy, leadership, process improvement, and software development. She is recognized for her performance in building collaborative leaders and teams that accelerate business performance within multiple industries, both for-profit and non-profit.

Then, after more than two decades of working in the corporate environment, she decided to start Vincerem to assist more leaders and organizations leverage their untapped potential.

Kim's passion is to coach great leaders and organizations through an integrated approach that build capabilities, which are foundational to the health and success of any organization. She believes all employees have an intrinsic purpose and set of strengths and, when leveraged, bring out exponential growth and productivity for themselves and any organization.

www.ingramcontent.com/pod-product-compliance
Lightning Source LLC
Chambersburg PA
CBHW030939180526
45163CB00002B/626